Get a Man, Keep a Man

Get a Man, Keep a Man

A Woman's Recipe for Love

Shei Atkins

authorHOUSE®

AuthorHouse™
1663 Liberty Drive
Bloomington, IN 47403
www.authorhouse.com
Phone: 1-800-839-8640

© 2010 Shei Atkins. All rights reserved.

No part of this book may be reproduced, stored in a retrieval system, or transmitted by any means without the written permission of the author.

First published by AuthorHouse 5/6/2010

ISBN: 978-1-4520-1879-9 (e)
ISBN: 978-1-4520-1877-5 (sc)
ISBN: 978-1-4520-1878-2 (hc)

Library of Congress Control Number: 2010906458

Printed in the United States of America
Bloomington, Indiana

This book is printed on acid-free paper.

Contents

Introduction	vii
1. Preparing For Marriage	1
2. Is He The One?	13
3. Letting Go of Pain from the Past	29
4. What If He Cheats?	37
5. Feeling Confident and Secure In Marriage	47
6. Don't Talk About It. Pray About It.	55
7. Keeping Your Man Interested In You Only	69
8. Stroking Your Man's Ego	79
9. Why Respect Is So Important	87
10. What Submission Really Means	97
About The Author	107
Thank You	111

Introduction

Have you ever had a desire to be married but became hesitant and fearful because of all the divorces and troubled marriages you have seen? Do you ever wonder how two people can promise to love each other for the rest of their lives and in just a few months or years down the line, they are heading for divorce? Have you ever wanted to know how to tell if a guy was the one for you? In this book, I will teach you about the qualities a man looks for in a wife and qualities that men do not want in a wife. You cannot expect to get Mr. Right while sending off signals for Mr. Wrong.

As a young woman, I have seen marriages come and go. I have seen people cheat on each other. I have seen women lose their husbands to other women. I have seen women disrespect their husbands. I have also seen people marry for the wrong reasons which later led to divorce. God put it on my heart to share the wisdom that I've learned about marriage to women. My heart never ceases to feel sorrow every time I hear a story about another divorce, infidelity in marriage, and homes being broken up. I really have a heart for women, and I desire to see my single and married sisters happy and wise. Many of us ladies go into marriage blindly. We go into marriage not really having a full understanding of what it encompasses. In this book, I will show you how to prepare for marriage; it is imperative that you learn all you can about the marriage covenant and being a wife. If you truly desire a husband and are asking God to send you a husband, then you have to prove it by becoming the person that fits what you want in life. In this book, I will also teach you how to know if a guy is the one for you or if you need to dismiss him. You will also learn what it takes to have a successful marriage and be the woman of your husband's dreams. Ladies, I pray that after you read this book, you will be more mature, have more wisdom on how to pick your men, and that your marriage will flourish because you have applied what you've learned in this book.

I

Preparing For Marriage

Before you prepare a meal, it is very important that you first have all the necessary ingredients to make the meal turn out the way the recipe intended. The same thing applies to preparing for marriage. There are certain ingredients that you should have to make it work. If you do not have all the right ingredients for marriage, now is your chance to find out what ingredients are missing and make it a priority to get them. Before you even think about walking down that aisle, there is a very important step that must not be overlooked. If you have any desire to be married you need to prepare for it. I have talked to many singles who desire to be married. A lot of them feel like they are ready for marriage and are just waiting on their husbands to show up. I must say that thinking that you are ready, and being ready are two different things. Waiting for your husband does not mean you should just sit there and look at your watch as if your work is done. Before you fall in love, it is very important that you put priority on spiritual, mental and emotional excellence. You cannot love someone else when you don't even love yourself. Don't wait until marriage to start dealing with your issues and excess baggage. There is always something to improve and the best time to do it is while you are single. If you desire to be married one day, you must understand that there are certain qualities that a man looks for in a wife. One thing that is sure to turn a man off is a **needy** woman. Neediness can be very irritating and is a negative quality in women. The reason that many women act like this in relationships is due to the fact that they have been neglected at some time in their lives and are afraid of it happening again. They do not want to experience this type of pain again. You cannot walk into a marriage that way. A man wants a woman who is **emotionally whole**. When you lack emotional wholeness, you look for your man to meet expectations that only God can meet. That will never be possible. No man can do God's job, so you cannot look for a man to fill your voids.

Another unattractive quality that will quickly turn a man off is a **gold-digger**. The gold-digging mentality is a mentality of the immature. 1 Corinthians 13:11 says, *"When I was a child, I spoke as a child, I understood as a child, I thought as a child: but when I became a man, I put away childish things."* If you desire to be married, you are going to have to do away with this kind of thinking. A gold-digger just wants a man with a nice car and plenty of money to give her while she shops all day and goes to the spa. A man wants a woman who has something going for herself. A man wants a ride-or-die woman who will hold him down through the good and the bad. Men do not want women who will use men for what they have. If a man gives a gold-digger the time of day, you better know that he is not looking for a wife in her. There is usually an exchange system in place and you know what is being exchanged for the money. So, if you are looking for a husband while holding on to a gold-digger's mindset, don't expect a quality man to love you and treat you like a queen. You are going to end up with a man who has no respect for women. God wants to give you a husband who will take care of you and love you like you need to be loved. But you will not get a man like that as long as you only want to take from the table without having something to bring to it.

Natural Wifey Qualities

Being a wife is more than having bling on your finger. A man wants a woman who respects herself. You can't disrespect yourself and expect a man to respect you. A man wants his woman to have a godly presence and carry herself like a lady. He wants a woman who doesn't just stimulate him physically but mentally as well. Men want graceful women, not women who are too headstrong and stubborn. They love classy women who are very intelligent. Men want women who are articulate and tactful, not loud women who will embarrass them in public. They do not want mouthy women who have problems submitting to authority figures either. If you cannot submit to authority figures, you definitely will not submit to your husband. A man can see that. He wants a mild-mannered woman. These are very attractive qualities that turn a man on and will surely grab the attention of a respectful man.

Emotional Wholeness

If you are not emotionally well, it is going to be very difficult to hold down a relationship, because once you get married, your problems are even more likely to be triggered because of the new levels of intimacy, responsibility and give and take required in marriage. You have to deal with your trust issues, control issues, jealousy, negativity, fears, and insecurities now. How can you love a husband without getting on his nerves when you have problems trusting men? How can you love a husband when you are so jealous that you think he wants every woman he gives a smile? How can you love a husband the way he needs to be loved when you are so scared he's going to leave you or cheat on you that you try to control his every move and end up pushing him away? Do you get my drift? So, you must prepare for marriage by understanding that there are certain qualities that a wife must have and there is a certain maturity level that one must have in order to hold a marriage together. You can compare preparing for marriage to preparing a delicious meal. There are certain ingredients you must have in order to have the desired results in a marriage. You and your future mate hold those very ingredients. The way your meal/marriage turns out depends on the quality of the ingredients. Not only must you have quality ingredients, but you must follow the God-given recipe.

Purpose of Marriage

One of the most important ingredients that you must have in this marriage recipe is Jesus. The reason why is because the marriage you desire is a physical representation of the relationship Jesus has with the body of Christ. Your relationship with your mate will only be as good as your relationship with God. You must know this going in because so many people marry for the wrong reasons and they get married without even knowing its purpose. When you don't know the purpose for something, you misuse it. If you do not have a relationship with God, you will not be able to display the very qualities you need in order to love your husband. Many marriages fail because they don't count up the cost of marriage. People go into marriage unprepared, and many unexpected circumstances and storms come that they were not ready to face. You have to go into marriage knowing that the devil hates it and he is going to come against it in every way. When you know this, you prepare your mind for battle beforehand. You go in with your mind already prepared to love your husband in spite of anything else. You build yourself up spiritually by reading the Word and growing closer to God. You need God and you need to know His voice. Without a close relationship with God, you will not be able to discern the wolves in sheep clothing that come for you. And trust me, they will come. You must also prepare for your husband by finding out what God has to say about love and then develop those qualities. God created marriage. So, what greater way is there to learn about it than from the designer himself?

Prepare To Love (Spiritual Qualities)

In order to love your husband the right way, you need to understand that love goes beyond a feeling. Feelings come and go; commitment doesn't. A husband is looking for a woman who is spiritually mature. A marriage has its share of ups and downs and if you do not choose to walk in love, it will not last. 1 Corinthians the 13 defines real love. These are qualities you need to work on developing now. It takes a real woman to love during the tough times in marriage.

> "Love is patient, love is kind. It does not envy, it does not boast, it is not proud. It is not rude, it is not self-seeking, it is not easily angered, and it keeps no record of wrongs. Love does not delight in evil but rejoices with the truth. It always protects, always trusts, always hopes, and always perseveres. Love never fails." 1 Corinthians 13:4-8.

Patience

Patience is a form of love that a wife must possess. Without it, your marriage will not work. Why, you ask? Because there will be times that your spouse will be weak in some areas that will get on your nerves. If you do not have patience to love him as he matures, you will give up on your husband. That is not how marriage works. Prepare for marriage knowing that you will suffer sometimes and be willing to stick through it.

Kindness

A good wife is not rude. She displays kindness no matter the situation. On a bad day, your husband might not display kindness toward you. That will be a time when he will need you to love him with kindness. Doing anything opposite will leave room for the enemy to come into your marriage and cause division. You have to be mature in Christ in order to be kind to someone when they are not kind to you. You cannot do it without God.

Meekness

Love is not prideful. You need to know this. There have been many times when my husband and I have argued and pride kept me from making up. Love does not hold grudges and I could do that with no problem. That doesn't work in marriage. Trust me. Pride makes you want to have the upper hand and it is selfish. Pride is a marriage assassin. Marriage is not for the prideful. In order to have a good marriage, you must be humble and kill your pride. When you kill your ego, the enemy has nothing to stroke. Prepare to be a humble wife.

Supportive

Love is not envious and it is not jealous. James 3:16, King James Version says: *For where envying and strife is, there is confusion and every evil work.* If you have envy and jealousy in your heart, trust me, it will manifest in your marriage. Trust and believe that where there is envy and jealousy, there is confusion and division in your relationship. You cannot love your husband and be jealous at the same time. Jealousy is the fear of losing something you love to someone or something else. Envy is a feeling of discontent or covetousness with regard to another's advantages, success, or possessions. These two are not exactly the same, but they are definitely related. Envy and jealousy will stop you from being happy for your spouse during promotions, and won't allow you to be happy for him during successes. If you have a problem with jealousy, you will be jealous of his job, time with friends, and anything you feel threatens the relationship. When you are struggling with the green eye within yourself, good things can happen for your spouse and instead of you being happy for him, you'll show lack of support and that is very destructive to a marriage. That is not love.

Selfishness

Selfishness is another marriage assassin. You cannot be selfish and think you are going to have a happy marriage. When you're single, you don't have to answer to anyone. You can come and go as you please. You can spend how you want to spend and stay out late if you choose to do so. When you get married, all that freedom stops. It is no longer I, but us. Your money becomes his money. Your account becomes his account. Your bills become his. I know you don't have a problem with that one. Your body becomes his body. You cannot spend like you are spending now. Marriage takes a lot of sacrifice and you will have to sacrifice a lot of the things you want in order to please your husband. Love isn't selfish. Love gives. You need to go into marriage ready to give, give, and give some more. If you think you are going to have a good marriage and be selfish, you are sadly mistaken. You are a helpmate to your husband and God is not giving you a husband so that you can change him or manipulate him into meeting your needs. Instead God wants you to minister to your husband.

Anger

Love does not act in anger. When you do not have control of your anger, you will do crazy, dumb, and immature things in marriage. When you are having a disagreement in a marriage, someone, if not both people, have to be the mature, or that thing will spiral into something that could have been prevented. I allowed my husband to get me so angry one time that I left my house and went to sleep in an empty apartment. That was so childish. I was hot and sweaty lying on a hard floor behind foolishness. It's funny now, but it sure wasn't funny then. I was the one suffering because I could not control my anger. I was the one who had to drop my pride and go back to apologize. I have grown tremendously since then. I am telling you this story to let you know that sometimes you do not know what's in you until you are faced with a situation. When you do not have a close relationship with God and don't know his Word, you will not be able to tame that anger that comes out of you. I have learned that the way you communicate with your spouse will determine the temperature of your marriage. If you want a nice loving marriage, it is imperative that you always respond to your husband in love, even when he is acting unlovely. Are you ready to do that? It takes a mature woman to love the unlovely.

Forgiveness

The longevity of every relationship is based on the willingness to forgive. In order to maintain any relationship, it is going to take forgiveness. There will be times your spouse will hurt you, whether spoken or in deed, and there will be times you hurt your husband. You can decide to give your flesh the satisfaction of holding a grudge, which will not get you anywhere. Or you can decide to forgive and walk in love, which will carry your marriage a long way. The bible says that *"love covers a multitude of sins."* That means more than one time. I told you that marriage is an example of the relationship between Jesus and the body of Christ. We hurt Him so many times and He still forgives us when we need it most. We have to display the same qualities to our husbands in our marriage relationships. Prepare to be a loving wife who has already decided in advance that she will forgive her husband.

Protect

Love does not delight in evil but rejoices with the truth. It always protects and always trusts. There will be times when your husband is going through something and might take it out on you when you have done nothing wrong. The bible says that love will not allow him to suffer and see it as payback for what he did to you. When angry, your flesh naturally does not want to communicate with your husband and will see him as an opponent. But that is not love. Love will see the best in him at all times. Love will see past what he did and see the pain he is going through. Love will protect him from looking bad in the eyes of other people. That really takes maturity. It takes a good wife to see that her husband would not intentionally hurt her. She is able to still protect his image when it comes to friends, family, etc. Prepare to protect your husband's image, love him in his suffering, and trust that everything will work out for the best.

Hope

Prepare to never give up hope in your marriage. If the enemy can make you give up hope in your marriage, he can make you lose the battle. Love always hopes, perseveres, and never fails. Winters will come in your marriage. Those will be the times that you must push through to the end. Prepare your mind to fight for your marriage at all costs. When you go into your marriage, go in knowing that there will be storms. Go in with an attitude to win and not lose. Go in knowing that real love does not fail. Prepare to love your husband in every way with an enduring love that is willing to suffer long.

Encouragement

God has a special someone for you and he is going to walk into your life at the appropriate time. Until then, instead of being discouraged about it, I encourage you to prepare for him by growing spiritually, physically, emotionally, mentally, and financially. The more whole you are as a person, the better your marriage will be. How's your credit? How do you spend money? Do you take care of yourself by staying in shape and eating healthy? How do you deal with conflict? Be the right person before you think about marrying the right person. Invest into your marriage now by investing into yourself.

Points to Remember

- ➤ Your relationship with your mate will only be as strong as your relationship with God.

- ➤ Before marriage, focus on spiritual, emotional, and mental wholeness.

- ➤ Men are looking for women who are respectful, classy, intelligent, smart, serve God, and not only have beauty but brains as well.

➢ Men are not looking to marry women who are gold-diggers, needy, controlling, not submissive, and immature.

➢ Waiting on your husband does not mean you should just sit and twiddle your thumbs. It is a time of getting closer to God, learning all you can about being a wife, the purpose of marriage, and preparing to love your husband the 1 Corinthians 13 way, and being patient until he comes.

Prayer

Heavenly Father,

I come to you recognizing you as my Lord and Savior. I know that you know what's best for me. I know you said that man wasn't meant to be alone, so I know that you have a man tailor made just for me, and I know that it will happen in your timing. Help me to be patient as I wait for my husband. Teach me to love the way you want me to love. Teach me what I need to know in order to be the wife my future husband needs. I let go of my old selfish ways. I no longer step ahead of you and choose wrong men because of my impatience. I want to be close to you God. I no longer settle for men who don't have my best interest at heart. Help me to be content in my singleness. I no longer depend on a man to make me happy, but I depend on you. I now understand that true happiness is found in you alone. From this point on, I am happy to give you complete control in every area of my life. In the name of Jesus, I pray, Amen.

2

Is He The One?

Knowing if a man is the one for you is a question to which you must have the answer before tying the knot. It's so essential. We as women are not in tune enough with the spirit and do not know how to discern when God is speaking concerning the men in our lives. We rely on our feelings more than the leading of the spirit of God.

Trust in the LORD with all your heart and lean not on your own understanding; In all your ways acknowledge him, and he will make your paths straight. Proverbs 3:5-6

Acknowledging God in all your ways is the only thing that ensures that you are walking the path God has laid out before you. You definitely cannot leave this out of the recipe. We have to acknowledge God in every area of our lives. We mess up when we lean to our own understanding and rely on our feelings to make choices. Feelings are so fickle. The Word of God is the truth and will never steer you wrong. Many people have failed at choosing the right mates because they did not know if the person they were dating was the one, or they had the answer and ignored the voice of the Holy Spirit when He said, "No." I know that since you are reading this book, you do not want to be another divorce statistic and you want to make the right choices in choosing your man.

What to Look For

There are certain characteristics in a man that immediately grab a woman's attention; from his looks, to the way he approaches you, to the way he speaks, to his personality. Look for someone who loves God before you look for beauty, muscles, popularity, or money. Knowing if a man is the one goes deeper than physical attraction and material things. Charm is also great, but charm does not mean that he is responsible. Before you even start dating, you want to find out if this man follows Jesus. You do not want a man who just says he is a Christian. You want a man who has the character and fruit to back it up. A man that has faith in God will base his life around his relationship with God and you will be able to see it. You're not looking for a perfect man, you are looking for a man who has a teachable spirit and has a desire to continually grow spiritually. That shows you that he will be willing to work on the marriage.

It is very important that you do not rush into a relationship. You want to take your time getting to know a man. As you spend time with him and learn more about him, you will begin to see more and more of his character. You are looking at how well he controls his temper. You are looking to see how he responds to disappointments. How does he treat those in authority? Does he treat you with respect, verbally, spiritually, and physically? You are looking for someone who can stand the heat. You do not want someone who will give up on you and the marriage the minute a storm comes. You are also looking at his maturity level. Maturity has nothing to do with age. I have seen many guys in their late forties and fifties who are very immature. You are looking for a man who is already ready to be an emotionally healthy and spiritually committed spouse. At the same time, don't have this huge list of unrealistic expectations that no man can meet. He will not be perfect, but he will be perfect for you. You do not have to be afraid of God sending you someone that you do not like. When God sends you someone, you will be attracted to him and you will love his dirty bath water. Well, maybe not that part. He might not be the best looking, but his personality will be so great that you won't even see that. Keep in mind that marriage has a godly purpose in the earth and being a wife is a ministry. God is giving you a man to whom you will love, serve and be a blessing.

How Will I Know If He's The One?

I want to start off by saying that any man who pulls you away from the will of God is not the one. Any man who is married and tells you that he is going to leave his wife for you is not the one. Any man who abuses you in any way is not the one. The God we serve has better for you and does not operate like that. Any man who does not respect you and still tries to sleep with you after you have told him that you are waiting until marriage is not the one. You want a man who respects your godly standards. I have learned that it is also a part of a man's game to act like he does not want to sleep you because he knows that it turns a woman on. Some men know that if they act like they don't want to have sex with you, then that will make you pursue and come on to them. Be on the lookout for those types of guys, and please do not fall for that. Anytime you date a man, you should ask God for discernment and ask him to unveil anything you need to know about this man's true character. Ask God to reveal anything you need to see about him that you cannot see now. God will speak to you concerning the men who come into your life because you are His child and He wants you to have his best. When you do not have that close tie with God and are very vulnerable and naive, a man will tell you anything and you will believe him. Men who are professional manipulators and liars know how to tell a woman what she wants to hear to get what he wants. Look out for wolves in sheep's clothing. You need to have a close relationship with God and know His voice. God speaks to us all in a way where we know he is speaking. We all are different. He will definitely speak to you in your inner-woman, which is your spirit. John 10:4-6 discusses God's sheep knowing His voice and not following any other voice. God speaks to me in dreams, so not only did I have inner peace in my spirit about my husband, but God spoke to me in dreams concerning my marriage and His desire for us. That is why it is so important to have that connection with the spirit. My husband and I fit together. We both do music. I sing and write, and so does he. He has produced all of my albums. We have the same desires and goals and pursue them together. God put us together because He has a purpose for us. We have a purpose that can only be fulfilled by us being together. I need him and he needs me. When God sends you someone, you will have similar goals and similar desires. You will both be special and unique, so you will sharpen each other in the marriage. God's purpose for your marriage might not be to reach the masses. But you will have a purpose to be a godly example to those around you and demonstrate the love of God. You will have a purpose to raise godly children and train them up in the Lord.

It is very important that you discuss all aspects of marriage with anyone you are dating who has the potential to be your husband. You also need to spend a sufficient amount of time together before even discussing marriage. You need to discuss issues such as morals, values, children, church affiliation; are you in agreement in these areas? You need to study God's Word together, especially the duties of a husband and wife which can be found in Ephesians 5:22-31, 1 Corinthians 7:1-16, Colossians 3:18-19, Titus 2:1-5 and 1 Peter 3:1-7; are there any red flags? Are you on one accord concerning spiritual doctrine? Do you both understand the purpose of marriage? Talk, Talk, Talk! Learn all you can about this man. Don't rush into anything! Make sure that you both have goals that move you in the same direction.

Red Flags

- He is unwilling to put the needs of another person above his own.

- He is not a forgiving person, easily offended, and holds grudges.

- He is mentally, emotionally and or physically abusive.

- He has an Unresolved Addiction Problem.

- He is not ready to commit.

- His career is the most important thing in his life.

- He is not equally-yoked with you or not saved.

- As a couple, you are not on one accord concerning handling finances, raising children and sexuality.

- He is not on your level but you think you can change him after marriage.

- You do not share the same values, goals, or interests.

If you see any of these signs in your partner, you might want to reconsider marrying him. When you enter into marriage, not only are you making a vow to your husband, you are making a vow to God, so it is not to be taken lightly. Go over this list with your man and discuss everything. Relationships fail when people ignore the red flags they see and still get married because they think the person will change. Who a person is as a single person is who they will be when they get married. If a man is not teachable and is selfish before marriage, more than likely, he is going to be selfish after marriage. There have been times when people got married to partners who were not saved, and they were able to win their spouses over to Christ, but this is not always the case, especially for those who know God did not authorize the marriage. What a person has done is the best indicator of what a person will do. Find out about the history of his past relationships. Why did they break up? What part did he play in the break up? Does he have children? Do they all have the same mother? Is he saved? Does he have a history of unfaithfulness? Do your homework and do not fall for anything that comes along and gives you some attention. Everything that glitters is not gold.

When God Says NO

You will make your heaven or hell on earth by the person you decide to marry. God sees things that we cannot see down the line. When he tells you a person is not the one, please listen. There are many people who know they heard the voice of God tell them not to marry a person and they did not take heed. They are having hell in their marriages at this very moment because they did not obey. The engagement period is a very crucial moment. You cannot be more fascinated with a wedding than you are with a marriage. It can get very bad when you have made it to the engagement and you still hear God saying, "Don't do it. He's not the one."

You may very well love this person. You've grown to love each other and you have become attached, and now you have to break it off. That is not easy to do when strong emotions and soul ties are involved.

When it comes to the point that you have fallen in love and you still hear that still small voice saying, "Don't do it. He's not the one," I truthfully have to tell you that you have inflicted this upon yourself. You saw the red flags early on. You heard God and you felt that uneasiness in your spirit about him. You did not have surety. Delayed obedience is disobedience, and when we fail to obey God when He first tells us to do something, we make it even harder for ourselves in the future. When you continue to grow in a relationship after God has said no, it is because you think that you can change this man after the wedding. It could also be that you really do not believe that God can send you something better. You feel that this is all you can get. When you really trust God and believe He has your best interest at heart, you will follow His voice. Disobedience costs and it backfires on us every time.

If you are reading this book and you know you hear God telling you to cut ties with someone because He has something better for you, please listen. There is a difference between being tested and tried by God and suffering behind our own foolish decisions. You must have the strength to be willing to end the relationship if you do not believe that marriage is the appropriate step. There is a reason that we do not go straight from the proposal to the chapel. The engagement period is for more than planning the wedding. This is the time that you think through what it means to be married and what it will be like to be married to this person. But when you believe very strongly that it is not going to work, you must build up the courage to call this wedding off. It is normal to worry about what friends and family may say. You may have to step outside the situation and push your feelings to the side in order to make the best decision. A small number of minutes or days of humiliation and hurt feelings are far easier to handle than months or years of a distressed marriage. This is one of the most significant decisions of your life, and you cannot let your concern about hurt feelings cause you to make an awful mistake.

Reasons God Says NO

- You are not ready (even if you "think" you are).

- Either one or both of you are marrying for the wrong reasons.

- You are unequally-yoked

- To protect you (God sees and knows what you don't).

- He is simply not the one for you.

When God says Yes

When God says yes, you have to start planning for your marriage along with planning for your wedding. Going into marriage without a plan is going in planning to fail. For the marriage to succeed you have to communicate, set goals, learn the proper skills, learn how to lead and follow, and share responsibilities. During this engagement process, you are learning how to deal with conflict together. You are learning how to disagree constructively before having children. It is very important that you are both on one accord spiritually and attend a church where you both can grow. Going to see a marriage counselor is a great idea if you want to help your relationship. If can be very effective if you go prior to any major long-term problems. You and your fiancé will be faced with many challenges in your marriage, and in many instances, you will have to rely upon your standards of faithfulness, truth, and goodness to see you through. If you find that you and your fiancé share many of the same standards, you will have a greater peace and pleasure in the years to come.

Go ahead and set the standard that divorce is not an option. Throw away that list of expectations that says, "If he (fill in the blank), I'm gone." That is the wrong mentality to have when it comes to marriage. You cannot go in already figuring out how you are going to exit the marriage if you become fed up with something he does. Some of you need to share the secrets that may cause you to lose trust in each other further down the road in marriage. Make sure you have done your emotional work before the wedding so you are equipped for the marriage.

Things to Discuss and Questions to Ask Before Marriage

1. How important to him is the celebration of special occasions such as birthdays, anniversaries, Valentine's Day?

2. What is his idea of "celebration?"

3. Should you (did you invite your exes to the wedding)?

4. Will you be allowed to go to lunch, dinner, or meetings with your ex?

5. How does he feel about you hanging with my friends? How often is too much? What is his way of being "romantic"?

6. Do you have a curfew? What happens if you come home late without calling?

7. How does he feel about having friends of the opposite sex while married?

8. What would he like for you to do specifically to show affection and care? (Really get down to specifics here, such as: I want you to greet me with a kiss when I come home. I'd like you to hold my hand in public; I'd like you to sit on the couch with me when we watch television).

9. In specified items, which is most important to him? Least important?

10. Anger (How do you both deal with it?). Can you live with how this person handles anger for the rest of your lives?

11. Do you agree on career choices?

12. Do you enjoy one another's appearance, sense of humor, attitudes toward life, achievements, personality, emotions, and habits of cleanliness?

If you have more 'No' than 'Yes' answers, consider whether or not you can overlook or tolerate these differences during a lifetime together.

More Checklist Questions to Consider

1. Are you both grounded in the word of God?

2. Can you freely discuss your Christian convictions?

3. Do you pray aloud with one another?

4. Will you stick around and support if one of you is called into ministry?

5. Do you agree to raise your children in a spiritual upbringing?

6. Do you enjoy hanging with other Christians?

7. Have you revealed memories of your childhood to your partner?

8. Are you outgoing or socially withdrawn?

9. Do you get along with your future in-laws?

10. Are you a good listener or do you tend to interrupt?

11. Would you listen to your parents over your fiancé?

12. Would you ever gossip to your parents about your fiancé's weaknesses?

13. Are you willing to give up your friends if your fiancé doesn't like them?

14. Do you agree politically?

15. Do you like to go out or are you a house cat?

16. What are your short- and long-term goals?

17. What are your spending habits?

18. Are you both willing to save money?

19. Do you like each other's driving?

20. Are you jealous if your fiancé appears to be more popular than you?

21. Are you patient?

22. How easily do you express affection?

23. Are you freely able to express intimacy?

24. Are you conceited or prideful?

25. What makes you cry?

26. Can you discuss your fears with your future mate?

27. Do you have any secrets you are afraid to discuss?

28. Can you adjust to each other's tempers?

29. Can you forgive your mate-to-be for any past wrong doing?

30. Are you still trying to please your parents?

31. When, if ever, do you feel jealous?

32. Can you tolerate his moodiness?

33. How would you handle temptation to cheat?

34. Do you ever blame anyone else for your mistakes?

35. How would you respond if your mate became severely ill?

You can sacrifice and take the time now to do the talking about your histories —where you come from and what you expect—or you can wait until those issues just show up. And they *will* show up. Along with talking about all these issues together, make sure you talk with God about them. Keep in mind that God is a creative God and will give you new, fresh thoughts if you ask Him. He is full of ideas! When the marriage is ordained by God, you can make it through anything together. Why go through storms with someone you were never supposed to be with? I LOVE being married to my husband, but I warn everyone preparing to get married. It won't be easy to combine your lives together and always approach life as a marital team. You will go through some storms together. You will have to make a lot of sacrifices to build your marriage into a good one. Don't overlook prayer and planning as you proceed very carefully into marriage.

Points to Remember:

- Pray about every man that you date.

- Look for someone who loves God before you look for beauty, muscles, popularity, or money. You do not want a man who just says he is a Christian; you want a man who has the character and lifestyle to back it up.

- Don't rush any relationship. Learning a person's character only comes through spending time together and do not ignore the red flags.

- When God says a man is not the one, even though you don't understand it, save yourself future troubles by obeying.

➢ You will make your heaven or hell on earth by the person you decide to marry.

➢ You cannot go into marriage with that "If he (fill in the blank), I'm gone" list. That means your marriage is doomed from the beginning. You never know what curveballs the enemy might use to attack the marriage.

➢ In marriage, you are building a life together, so go into it knowing that the enemy will attack, but make the decision that you are going to stick with your husband for better or for worse.

Prayer

Dear Heavenly Father,

I come to you leaning not to my own understanding. I trust in you with all my heart and I acknowledge you in all my ways. I ask that you direct my path concerning the person I'm currently in a relationship with. I ask that you speak to me concerning this man. I ask you to remove any blinders I have on my eyes concerning the man I'm dating. Give me discernment to see his true motives. My desire is to be in your will and I know that the people I connect with should sharpen me and push me to better. If the man I'm dating is not the one for me, please give me the strength to cut all ties and let him go. Forgive me for not listening to you at first when you told me not to go any further with him. If he is the one you have for me, I ask that you strengthen us to live holy before you until the wedding. My desire is to please you. I choose to make you number one in this relationship. I know that you are the creator of marriage and it is a physical representation of the relationship between Jesus and the body of Christ. My desire is to display the love of God, patience, and kindness in my marriage. My desire is to walk in the fruit of the spirit concerning my marriage. I make up in my mind now to love this man. I make up in my mind now to build him up and not tear him down. I know that every marriage has storms, so I make up in my mind to love him and stick it through for better or for worse. Thank you for placing him in my life. I give you the glory and the praise in Jesus name, Amen.

3

Letting Go of Pain from the Past

An important part of this recipe for love is letting go of pain from the past. Have you ever cooked spaghetti before? If you have, I'm sure you are familiar with a grease strainer. The grease strainer drains as much of the accumulated fat from the meat as possible. When cooking, everything is not meant to go into the pot. Some things have to be done away with to make sure the meal turns out the way it should. The same thing goes with your successful marriage recipe. In order to let go of pain from the past, you are going to have to drain a lot of things that will have a negative effect on your marriage. Everything that you have experienced from childhood until now has shaped you into who you are today. Some things have affected you positively and some negatively. Your life is like a stage play. You might not have been able to control where you were born, the type of parents you had, the abuse, the foster homes, the molestation, the rape, and the rejection. But guess what? You do have a choice in how your character responds. You get to write the script of your character.

What role has your character been playing? No matter what script you have written for your character so far, from this point on, you have a choice to make it better. No matter what pain you have experienced in your life from this point until now, it's time to let go. It is time to let go so you can heal. It is time to leave the baggage of the past at the feet of Jesus once and for all.

You do not want to carry this into your new marriage. When you are not healed, depending on the trials of your past, you become more of a burden. You become more like a child to raise. When you are not healed, issues surface and affect how you treat and respond to your spouse. When you are not healed, when these issues surface, your spouse has to cater to these issues instead of enjoying you. I can recall being molested as a child. I was molested by family and I was molested by friends of the family. I never realized how it affected me until I got married. It tore down how I felt about myself. It made me feel like what I had to offer wasn't good enough. It created a fear in me that I have carried since I was a child. Not only that, I grew up in a home of physical abuse and divorce. So on top of feeling insignificant because of the sexual abuse, I experienced the pain of a broken family. It created an emptiness and sadness in me. I grew up seeing myself beneath everyone. I grew up with fear of rejection.

I grew up lacking self-worth. I was very sensitive, and I still am in certain areas. I was very defensive and my feelings were hurt very easily. I felt unworthy because of what I went through, so I always thought people were out to get me. I always thought people were out to tear me down when that was not the case. It's like I was looking for what was familiar to me. I was looking for people to hurt me. That's what I expected. And guess what? I carried those same feelings into my marriage. So when my spouse said something to me, my feelings were hurt. I would jump on the defense and attack back when I wasn't really attacked. This created tension in my marriage because I was not healed. It made me treat the very man who was trying to love me like someone off the street who did not care about me. If you grew up without your parents or in a single-parent home, you were rejected by your parent and sometimes it creates a fear of being rejected by other people, including your spouse. It also causes you to put up a wall to "protect" yourself from being hurt again. Imagine if I had married someone who did not have my best interest at heart. They would have left me a long time ago. That's why it is so important to marry someone who loves God and is able to love you with patience when you aren't just acting a fool, but *reacting* a fool. I have come to learn that letting go is a process. Please know the importance of working on yourself before marriage. Don't get me wrong, no one is perfect, but when you deal with your issues before marriage, it prevents you from going through so many unnecessary problems that could make or break the marriage. Even if you went into your marriage with issues you have not dealt with, now is your time to be free. It may have taken me a long time to identify and get to the root of my issues, but I have developed three keys to help you let go of the past so you can go ahead and move forward and experience the joy and freedom God desires for you.

Identify and Forgive

Take a moment and think about your past for a second. Think about what is holding you back from experiencing and giving love. What is hindering you in your relationships? What is hindering you from being all God called you to be? Is it fear? What issues have surfaced from within you that keep you from moving forward? Is it jealousy? Is it negative thinking and insecurity? Is it anger? Is it self-sabotage? Is it low-self-esteem? Is it unforgiveness? Think back on every person who has hurt you that you have not yet forgiven. Think back on everyone who you have hurt. Just go back in your mind and think about why you feel the way you feel. Think about what happened to you to make you think so low of yourself. Think about the hurtful words that were spoken to you that made you feel so insecure. Think about the rejection you experienced that made you feel you are not good enough so you settle for anyone who gives you attention. Think about what drastic situation created such fear in you. Also think about how it is negatively affecting you now.

Now, I want you to picture yourself wrapped in chains from your shoulders to your feet. Picture the faces of the people who hurt you. See the faces of your abusers. See the face of the person who raped you. See the face of the father who was never there. See the face of the friends who betrayed you. See the face of your past boyfriend or husband that cheated on you and broke your heart to pieces. After you have gone back into your mind and identified the causes of all your pain I want you to picture one more thing. I want you to picture the lock of the chains in one of your hands. I want you to picture that lock being open. Continue to see the faces of all those people who hurt you. Whether you believe it or not, some people need to forgive a place that reminds them of the pain. Say out loud, "I forgive you." I also need you to forgive yourself and know that what they did to you was not your fault. If they never say I'm sorry, you still have to forgive them. It is for your own freedom. Say, "I release you now for what you did to me once and for all." If you need to forgive God, do it. Forgive God because you feel like if He was really there for you, He wouldn't have let it happen. God did not do it to you, sis. Man has free will. You have to overcome this thing, because there are others who you will come across who have been through the same thing you went through, and they are going to need you to tell them how you did it. Even if you did something that made you so shameful that guilt has taken over your life, it is time to let it go now, Sis. You are new in Christ. The old has passed away. See your freedom happening in your mind. Release the lock and chains from your hands and see them unraveling as gravity pulls them to the floor. You are free. You were the one holding yourself back all this time. It is called self-imprisonment. Bitterness is an acid that hurts the object in which it is stored more than the object on which it is poured. This is exactly what happens when you hold on to hurt from the past. You hurt yourself more than the person you are bitter toward. You cannot be a successful wife while holding on to the pain of your past.

Change and Realize

After you have identified where the bitter fruit in your life has come from and forgiven the people who have betrayed and abused you, it is time to change the way you think about others' actions. Jesus said that He came to set the captives free, and one of the areas that we all have to be set free from is some of the wrong thinking that was birthed out of the negative experiences which occurred in our pasts. There were reasons that the people who hurt you made the choices they did, even if you do not understand or even know what those reasons were. God is ready to do a new thing in your life, but he cannot do it without your permission. It is time to appreciate and start loving yourself again. It is time to know your self-worth. Those walls that you put up have been keeping you from receiving the fullness of love that those who really care about you have been trying to give you. You need to realize that everybody is not out to get you. People actually care and love you very much. You are special and unique and you need to see it. You can either choose to stay fully bound up in your past, continue to throw pity parties and blame everyone and everything for your miseries, or you can choose to rise up and make a brand new start with the Lord by choosing to fully surrender your entire life into His hands. Work with God to get your past fully cleaned up so that you can wholly start to live in the present and move into the call and destiny that He has already planned out for you. Refuse to allow those past memories to hurt you again. Realize that letting go is a process and that you have to take this thing one day at a time. You are moving forward with a new attitude and a new mindset. You understand now that the enemy wanted to destroy you a long time ago and you are not going to allow him to succeed because you are a changed woman.

Accept and Know

You have identified the root issues and forgiven. You have realized that you can do nothing to change the past, but you can change yourself. Now it is time to accept that the past is over and understand that your future is your responsibility. Commit to making your life as good as it can be. Know that sometimes these issues will try to resurface at times but that doesn't mean you did not forgive. Who you have become today did not happen overnight, so you won't be perfect and whole overnight. But when these issues creep up sometimes, that is only life's way of showing you that you are still human. That is life's way of showing you to never get comfortable. Romans 12:1 says, *"Present your body daily as a living sacrifice, holy and acceptable unto God."* It goes on to say that the only way you can be transformed is by renewing your mind with the Word of God. You cannot be changed handling things the way the world handles it. The world tells you to get revenge. The world says, "If you hurt me, I'm going to hurt you." But that is not God's way. You can never change doing what comes natural to the flesh. Change always costs something that you do not naturally want to do to get something that you really need and want. Letting go will be the best thing that can ever happen for you and for your marriage.

Points to Remember

- ➤ Even though you had no choice in your parents, your childhood and the abusive parents, you do have a choice and are responsible for who you become.

- ➤ No matter where you are in your life right now, it is never too late to start working on yourself.

- ➤ When you are not healed, issues surface that affect your marriage in a negative way.

- ➤ You need to deal with the root issues to take care of the fruit issues in your life.

- ➤ Let go by first identifying what is hindering you from moving forward and forgive yourself and anyone else who had a part in your pain.

- ➤ You must change any negative thoughts you have that are a result from your past and realize that letting go is a process that you have to take one day at a time as you move forward with your new attitude and new mindset.

- ➤ Accept that the past is over and understand that your future is your responsibility. Know that every now and then that God will allow certain things to surface, but it does not mean you did not forgive. It is just showing you what you need to work on and shows that you are human.

- ➢ None of this can be done without the help of God. Include prayer and worship in this process of letting go.

Prayer

Dear Heavenly Father,

I recognize you as my all in all. I have learned that everything I need can be found in you. My desire is to please you in every area of my life. I'm ready to move forward in my life and there are so many issues that are hindering me. God, I ask you to heal me of the pain I have inside. Heal me from the inside out. Lord I've had this wall up so long that I don't even know how to take it down. I ask you to create in me a clean heart and renew the right spirit in me. The abuse, the betrayal, the lies, the molestation, and the rejection have made me feel so insignificant and worthless. I have anger inside of me and I'm ready to let go. Forgive me for holding on to this anger so long because I couldn't forgive. I know that I can't do this without you and I don't want to. Heal me emotionally. The pain has stressed me so bad that it is affecting my health. I ask that you heal me physically as well. I receive your healing. Shower me with you love and care God. Manifest your awesome presence. Draw me closer to you and help me to recognize who I am in you. I cancel every assignment of the enemy on my life now. I bind the spirit of fear from operating in my life. I bind every spirit of anger in my life. I lose your power and love in my life. I lose godly wisdom over my life. I lose understanding in my life and I lose joy and peace. I know that everything I've been through is working for my good because I recognize that I am called according to your purpose. Help me to love myself. Make me a strong woman of God that can be an example to others around me and help me to be the kind of wife that makes her husband proud. In Jesus name I pray, Amen.

4

What If He Cheats?

Sometimes when you really don't feel like cooking a meal, you try to cook it as quickly as possible. How many of you know that quick is not always good? When you try to cook fast, sometimes you leave out or don't put enough of a certain ingredient into it. It could be because you were tired or you weren't in the mood. When infidelity arises in a marriage, you better believe somebody left out some ingredients. A guard was let down. A bad ingredient got into the marriage recipe. Somebody left an open door for the enemy to come in. Somebody failed to use the drainer on their thoughts and allowed the enemy to infiltrate their life, which affected the marriage. Being cheated on is one of the biggest fears that women have not only when it comes to marriage but just relationships period. Based on university research, psychological surveys, mass public polls and the recordings of marriage and family counselors; 41% of one or both spouses have admitted to emotional infidelity and 57% of men have admitted to infidelity in every relationship they have had. Infidelity is very serious. As a wife, you cannot scare or threaten a man to keep him from cheating. You can't stop a person from doing anything. Being that I have experienced infidelity in my marriage I do want to let you know that even though infidelity is grounds for divorce, it does not have to be the reason for divorce. If you have experienced physical or emotional infidelity in your marriage, my heart breaks for you and I want you to know that there is hope for you. Marriages can heal. I am a living witness that you can make it through it. If my husband and I were able to survive it, you can, too.

I remember when the news hit me. It felt like someone took my heart and just shattered it to pieces. The pain was so horrible; I wouldn't wish it on anyone. I knew something was about to hit. I just didn't know what. I talk about having that connection with God because when you do not have it, you will not hear or know His voice when He speaks to you. I am a woman of prayer and worship, so I remember being in prayer and God spoke to me. I heard Him so clearly. He said, "The devil wants your husband." He told me to pray for him 30 minutes a day. That's all I knew. I found myself reading a lot of marriage books and just praying for my husband not knowing what was about to hit. About two months later, everything hit the fan. But guess what? Because I had that relationship with God and made up in my mind from the beginning that divorce was not an option, I handled my husband the same way that God handles me when I fall. Listen to me, Sis. If God told you to marry this man, don't leave. God did not change his mind about him being your husband just because he cheated. You know what I have learned? Sometimes your husband has to grow into the man that you prayed and asked God for. If your husband is truly sorry for what he did and not just sorry he got caught, give him another chance.

I remember being at church and my pastor's wife was preaching on marriage. She said if your friend called you and told you that her husband cheated on her and she needed your encouragement and wanted prayer, what would you do? All the ladies in the congregation said they would be there for their friend. She then asked, "If you can do this for your friend, why wouldn't you do that same thing for your own husband if he cheated?" I never forgot that statement. I was able to draw strength from those words during my suffering. Even though my husband betrayed me, I built him up because he was very remorseful for what he did. He wasn't just sorry he got caught. That is what love does. I forgave my husband, and I prayed with my husband. Guess what else? I continued to sleep with him through the pain. I cried sometimes, but I did it because that is my duty as a wife in spite of what storms come in the marriage. All I could see was him and another woman in my head but I still loved him in my actions through it all. NOTHING but the power and grace of God helped me make it through it. Sis, if you still want your marriage, God will help you through this.

When you find out your husband has cheated, it feels like the weight of the world is crushing down on you. Your heart is pounding and filled with anxiety. It's hard to think straight. Every ounce of trust you had for your husband is gone. And you have to fight with every ounce of strength you can muster to keep your flesh from having its way in the situation. You will want to get revenge. Your will want to just leave him high and dry. You will want to curse him and just jump on him and just start punching him every time you see him. That's the truth. In order to win this battle, you must draw strength from 1 Corinthians 13, the love chapter.

Affairs can strip a woman of her self-esteem and cause insecurity. It is a tactic of the enemy to make you feel guilt and think that it was your fault. Affairs also create insecurity in you because you feel like you weren't good enough for your husband for him to go outside the marriage and choose another woman over you. That is a lie from the enemy. Whether or not you and your spouse reconcile, it is important for you to give yourself the right to grieve. You have been through a terrible disloyalty. Don't let anyone convince you otherwise. You have been hurt and those feelings of betrayal and heartache are common and to be expected. However, it is imperative that you take those feelings of hurt to the Lord and allow Him to minister to you and nurse you back to health.

There were days and nights I cried and cried. There were many nights I cried myself to sleep. There were nights that the enemy told me just go and get sloppy drunk. Every day I bowed on my face before God and prayed for healing. I hated the pain I was feeling. I said, "God, my desire is to please you but my flesh is telling me to go get revenge. Please hold me." I said, "God, please anoint me to make it through this because I don't want to let you down." God knew my pain and every time I prayed, His presence came into that room so strong and God just held me in His arms. You cannot make it through the pain of infidelity without prayer. The recovery is so painful. But 2 Corinthians 12:9 says, *"But He said to me, 'My grace is sufficient for you, for my power is made perfect in weakness."* God has made a promise that his grace is sufficient for you and during this time of weakness, His power will be made perfect in your life.

I was constantly on a seesaw with my emotions during this time. I really learned how to rely on God for my happiness and strength. If you are reading this and dealing with the betrayal of your husband cheating on you, I want to let you know that God did not cause this negative situation. It is easy to get into the trap of blaming God. God knew it was going to happen, but He didn't cause it. The same way God needs a body to use to do His work in the earth realm, the enemy does, too.

The enemy can do nothing without a person allowing him to use them. You might think it would be easier to handle if you just get rid of your husband. After all, the Bible does allow for divorce concerning this area. You have to sit and really think. Would a divorce be better? Listen, don't trade your husband in on the chance that you will get a husband who does not make mistakes. I know that God is able to bring good out of the pain and hurt you are facing.

The Wall

One thing that we as humans do after being hurt by someone is put up a wall. We never want to experience pain like it again. So, what we do is put up this wall over our hearts. The wall is meant to protect us so that if it happens again, we will be okay because we expected it and were prepared for it. It sounds like the right thing to do, but that is totally opposite of how we should respond. That wall keeps us from giving our heart again and it keeps us from receiving the love we need. Not only does this wall keep us from giving and receiving love from our spouses, it also keeps us from giving and receiving the fullness of God's love as well. That wall says, "God, I can't trust that you'll protect me so I have to protect myself." As time passed, I found myself not wanting to sleep with my husband because I could not allow myself to be vulnerable and give my heart to my husband again. This was the hardest part of my marriage because I had this wall up and I could not trust my husband. I forgave him but the trust was gone. I told myself I would never experience that kind of pain again and put my guard up. Our relationship was great until it was time to go to bed. I was not the same woman. I was bitter on the inside. My husband could only go so far with my heart. I would lock and curl myself up in a sleeping position so that if he tried to touch me, he would have a hard time hitting the hot spots. If he could get me hot, we were able to be intimate, but if I could help it, he wouldn't be able to get to the spots. If you find yourself doing what I did, let me tell you something, losing sexual desire for your husband is the worst thing you can do to tear a man down. Men love to feel needed, admired, and most importantly, be intimate with their wives. If your husband truly loves God and made the mistake of cheating on you, imagine how he feels about what he did. He feels guilty. He feels terrible. He feels unworthy, embarrassed and full of shame. God knows that you are afraid of being hurt again, but He wants you to keep trying. It is during these rough times that you must really seek God and allow him to heal you. You are going to have to be open to love your husband the way he needs to be loved. Why? At the end of the day, marriage is a physical manifestation of our relationship with Jesus and the church. When we sin against Christ and ask for forgiveness, He forgives us and loves us with an unconditional love. That is the same love we must give our husbands when they mess up.

Trust

Infidelity destroys all trust for your husband. Distrust destroys passion in a marriage. When passion is lost in a marriage, it is only a matter of time before you find your marriage on life support. And it is going to take doings on both of your parts to nurse it back to health. Even though you have chosen to forgive your husband, now you have to really learn how to trust your husband all over again. Trust is not something that happens just because we forgive. The same way you chose to forgive your husband, you are going to have to choose to trust him. There will be many days and nights when your husband is not home that you'll wonder if he is out cheating on you. Those are the times you will have to pray and ask God to help you not assume that your husband is out with another woman. By you showing that you trust your husband, he will prove to be more trustworthy. When you are in the trust-building stage after infidelity has occurred, as much as you want to go off and start accusing your husband if he comes home late, don't do it. Acting out, pointing fingers, assuming, and accusing makes your husband think and feel that things will never get right between you two. You might be reading this and feeling like you have to do all the work and that I'm not saying anything to the men about what they did. You are correct. This chapter is for wives who have been cheated on that want to know if and how they can survive something so horrible. Can you understand why it is so important to have a close knit relationship with God and His word before entering a marriage? You cannot love your husband the way God loves without being strong and mature in Christ. It takes a mighty strong woman in God to love her husband after he has cheated on her. It takes a strong woman to pray for her husband and still take care of his needs after he has betrayed her. It takes a very strong woman in Christ to still sleep with a man who has hurt her.

Good marriages are not an accident. They don't just happen. I have learned that a couple must decide to stay together and work at the marriage no matter how hard life gets. Adultery is one of the hardest tests a marriage could ever face. But guess what? In God's eyes, adultery is sin like any other sin. God puts every transgression in the same category… sin. Jesus died to provide forgiveness for our sins. Forgiveness and trust are a choice. No one can earn forgiveness; it has to be given freely. If you are having a hard time letting go, keep on praying until you are able to truly forgive. You will feel bitterness and anger flare up at times. That is when you are to pray and release those hurtful feelings over to God. Ask Him to help you. As long as you have the desire to forgive and trust your husband again, God will help you.

If you are considering leaving your husband, realize that even another marriage with another man does not mean that this will never happen to you again. When you divorce one man and marry another one, the wounds take years to heal. We hoodwink ourselves into thinking that we are going to find "Mr. Perfect" and combine our families into one big, happy element with no struggle. I encourage you to take every ounce of strength you have on hand to make your marriage work. Never enable sin or selfishness, but live like Christ with every fiber of your being. If you are already divorced, take heed. If there is any way to resolve the situation, pray that the Lord will give you the guts to obey. If you are on your second or third marriage, God will give you a dose of His grace that will bring healing and wholeness to your past. I do not believe that divorce is God's perfect will, but I do believe God takes us where we are and moves us forward. He forgives and holds us up in His unfailing love.

Points to Remember

- ➢ You cannot scare or threaten a man to stop him from cheating. People do what they want to do.

- ➢ Even though infidelity is grounds for divorce, it does not have to be the reason for divorce.

- ➢ God did not change his mind about him being your husband just because he cheated.

- ➢ Sometimes your husband has to grow into the man that you prayed and asked God for.

- When dealing with your husband after infidelity, treat him the same way Christ treats you when you fall. That is our Christian duty.

- Divorcing and remarrying does not make you immune to this happening again.

- Know that God can and will heal your marriage and that His grace is sufficient for you during this time.

- Forgive your husband and make the choice to trust him again by relying on the strength of God.

- If Jesus demonstrates His unconditional love to us and forgives us when we're unfaithful to Him, who are we to withhold that same unconditional love and forgiveness from our spouses?

Prayer

Dear God,

I am hurting so bad right now. I pray that you will reawaken the love I once had for my husband. God I ask that you will give me a new vision of what my marriage can be. I am asking that you give me the strength to do everything in my power to resurrect what you originally ordained. Lord I really want to do something horrible to my husband and I need you to give me the desire to forgive. Lord you know that I am struggling with wanting to retaliate, but my greater desire is to please you. Lord, remind me that you died for him just like you died for me. Give me the intensity of love that freely extends forgiveness. God, I ask that you will remove the influence of every woman my husband has slept with from our marriage. God, give me the courage I need to travel this pathway of forgiveness. My desire is to please you. God, I run to your secret place. Hide me under your shadow. You are my fortress. Revive my broken spirit. Let your power take control as I yield to your spirit. I pray that my marriage will be an example of the love of God to many people. You get the glory out of this situation and let it work together for my good. In Jesus name I pray. Amen.

5

Feeling Confident and Secure In Marriage

Confidence and security play major roles in the recipe for love. Without these two ingredients, you cannot be the kind of wife you need to be to your husband, depending on the areas you lack confidence. *Confidence* is a firm belief in your own power, abilities, or capacities. Security is being free from fear and anxiety. Your confidence is affected by your beliefs. Every single thing that has happened to you has helped you form a picture of the world. Some experiences made you realize what you were capable of. Other experiences made you realize what you weren't capable of. For example, when you were a young child, if your best friend or sibling made better grades than you, you might have formed the belief that you were not very smart. On the other hand, if you made better grades than your best friend or sibling, you might have formed the belief that you were very smart. Over time, these experiences add on top of each other to become beliefs. These beliefs determine how we look at ourselves and the world.

In the example I just mentioned, can you see how the fact that your friend made better grades than you determined your appraisal of yourself? The fact is that the good grades your friend made has no actual impact on the grades you made, but it did have an effect on how you felt about yourself. And it had an effect because beliefs are often more related to interpretation than fact. The amazing thing about beliefs is that they have an unsubstantiated link to reality. It's all about how you interpret that reality. This explains how two people with the same level of ability can have two totally different views of themselves. They have each chosen to interpret their reality in a different way. This applies to your beliefs about confidence. Being confident in marriage will have less to do with your actual abilities but more often your interpretation of previous events in your life. When you don't have confidence in yourself, it will affect your marriage. Why? You can't give what you don't have. You will be easily offended in areas where you are not confident. You can have confidence in some areas and not be confident in other areas. It is very important to be a confident wife and be secure in your abilities. In order to please your husband, you have to have confidence in yourself. If you are not confident, you will question and second guess every positive thing he says about you. You do not need another person to make you feel special. You should have confidence in who you are and what you bring to the marriage.

A woman's self-confidence affects her thoughts, feelings, behavior, and body. When a woman has low self-confidence, she does not think she can do anything. When a woman is not confident in her looks, the minute another beautiful woman walks past her husband and she sees him looking at her, she immediately feels less of a woman. Likewise, when a woman is not confident in her cooking, she will start feeling threatened as soon as her husband tastes another woman's food and likes it. Any area you lack confidence, you will feel insecure when you see another woman doing it well.

Instead of rejoicing with her, you'll be jealous. Remember the best friend example with the good grades? That's what happens when you do not have confidence in yourself. Although your cooking, your body, your hair and IQ level might be great, you will not perceive it that way when someone just as gifted as you steps on the scene. Know who you are and what you have to offer. When you are on top of your game, you can learn to celebrate another woman's strengths instead of feeling threatened by them. Your husband wants you. If he wanted those other women, he would have married them. But he didn't; He married you. So be the best you that you can be.

I remember I once did not have a lot of confidence in myself. I wasn't confident in how I looked and I wasn't confident in my abilities. So every time a beautiful woman came on the scene, I would always acknowledge her first just to let my husband know that I see her and I'm watching him to see if he is looking, too. I know I am not the only woman who has done this. I have learned that there will always be beautiful women around and because men are visual, they are going to look. That does not mean he wants her. See, it's all about perception and interpretation. At first my interpretation was that he was looking because he wanted her or she looked better than me. I was not secure in myself. That's why I had those feelings. Since I have dealt with those issues and matured, my perception now is that men are visual and I know that they will look at other women. Women look at other men as well. But I know that he is coming home with me. He loves me. It is not until you become confident in yourself that you can be secure in the marriage. See ladies, you have to know that no other woman can do it like you. No other woman can beat you doing you. That is what I had to grow to learn and understand. I also had to learn how to be secure within my gifts. I am a singer and my voice is different from others. I used to be so insecure when I got around other singers who had strong powerful voices like Patti Labelle and Fantasia that make people stand to their feet. I felt like when I sang, nobody stood up. I felt like I didn't get that response. I was looking at the wrong thing. The person who seeks acceptance is controlled by the people he or she wants to please. I should sing because I love it and not to get a certain response out of people. When you envy what other people have, you do things for the wrong reasons and there is no purity in that. When you are not secure within yourself, you start competing and making bad decisions to keep up with others. Be you. Love yourself and be confident. You can never appreciate what you have to offer focusing on what other people have. That is exactly what I was doing. Now I know what I have to offer and what God created me to be. God gave me a soft, unique, pretty voice. I have an authenticity about me and transparency about me that captures my audience's attention and a soft pure voice that speaks to the souls of men. I couldn't see that at first. Now I know who I am and I am so in love with myself. Now I can give my husband the love that he deserves. Do you know who you are? Do you realize that you do not have to covet what somebody else has because what you have is so unique? I need you to see it. You can be the best to your husband when you know that you are the best. Let me give you three keys that have helped me and will help you develop confidence and security in yourself and in your marriage.

Focus on and Appreciate Your Strengths

Self-confidence is like a bank account; you need to make regular deposits into it to keep it growing. People who have a lot of self-confidence focus on what their strengths are, not on what they cannot do. There is no one else like you in this world. No one looks like you, has the same talents, experiences or perspective as you do. You are unique and are, therefore, here to make your unique contribution. If we each focus on what we bring into the world to share, there can be no comparisons, jealousy or regret. Everyone has things that need improvement and things they are not good at, but the difference is that not everyone dwells on them. Recall and appreciate everything you have accomplished so far in life. Think about everything you love about yourself and what makes you who you are. Did you finish college? Are you very smart? Did you accomplish a lot with no college degree? Did you overcome some tough challenges in your life? Do you finish what you start? Are you a successful mother? Do you cook very well? Do you make your husband happy? Are you great with money? Make a list of your strengths today and focus on things you do well. Recollect your past successes, distinctive skills, loving relationships, and positive momentum. You will be surprised how much you have going for you and will be motivated to take that next step towards success. When you are focused on yourself and what you want to do in life, you have no time to worry about what everyone else is or isn't doing. Your husband deserves a confident woman and you owe it to yourself.

Exercise

Along the same lines as personal appearance, physical fitness has a huge effect on self-confidence. If you are out of shape, you will feel insecure, unattractive, and less energetic. When you are in shape, you will feel sexier, dress sexy, and walk with confidence. When you don't feel attractive, it can affect your sex life with your husband. I remember gaining 30 pounds earlier in my marriage. I couldn't be free with my husband sexually like I wanted to be because I was too worried about cellulite here, a roll over there, and a big stomach. So guess what I did? I lost the weight. Now I like how I look and how I feel, and I know my husband likes the new and more confident me. Your husband wants you to be sexy for him. He wants you to wear sexy lingerie, not big grandma underwear. To dress provocatively in the "bedroom" generally means that the clothing is ultimately going to come off. When your self-image is low, you will not feel comfortable doing that. Some women don't like to go out with their husbands because they do not feel beautiful and would rather save their husbands the embarrassment by staying home all the time. Your husband does not deserve this. What happened to woman he used to have fun with? What happened to the spontaneous side of you? It is time to refresh your marriage. That can only happen by you refreshing yourself. Join a gym. Build confidence by taking care of your body and losing those extra pounds. All it takes is a little bit of investing into yourself. It has been found that the lack of self-love is often the root causes of conditions like eating disorders, obesity or even terminal diseases. By working out, you improve your physical appearance, energize yourself, and accomplish something positive. Having the discipline to work out not only makes you feel better, it creates positive momentum that you can build on the rest of the day.

Never Stop Learning and Growing

There is something about setting goals and accomplishing them that gives you a sense of self-worth. You never want to get to the point where you stop growing. When you stop growing, it's easy to start thinking negatively about yourself. Know who you are and what you want. As has been said so many times, "If you don't know where you are going, how will you know when you get there?" Take the time to figure out what your strengths, aptitudes and capabilities are and how you can best use them to achieve personal satisfaction and fulfillment. Make a deliberate attempt to look for opportunities that can help improve your sense of self. For instance, if you are particularly good at doing something, set aside more time to indulge and improve your skills on it. Knowing that you have particular gifts can boost your self esteem. Continue to assess and evaluate yourself. Self-confidence can rise and fall depending on what you are doing with yourself. If you happen to slack off and choose not to keep improving, you will begin to feel uninspired and less confident.

What do you want to do? If you are insecure in your marriage, what can you do to build confidence? Learn something new. You might be a stay home mom who feels like all you're good for is taking care of the house or kids. What you can do is take up a course in something you have always wanted to learn or go back to school. It's never too late to do something as long as you are still alive. The more you learn and the more you accomplish, the more confident you become. So instead of complaining about where you are in life, do something about it. It's all about you right now. This is your time for joy, peace, and happiness. It is time to invest into your marriage by investing into yourself. Always speak positively about yourself and speak life into yourself. Stop pointing out every negative thing and eliminate self-criticism. The bible says that life and death are in the power of the tongue, so speak life. You are a very important part in this recipe for love and we don't need any incomplete ingredients. God wants you to have the kind of marriage that represents him well. This chapter is all about knowing who you are and knowing what you have to offer. Walk into who God called you to be.

Points to Remember

- ➤ Your confidence is affected by your beliefs. Change your beliefs about yourself to build your confidence.

- ➤ You do not need another person to make you feel special. You should have confidence in who you are and what you bring to the table of life.

- ➤ When you are so busy looking at what other people have, you cannot appreciate what you have to offer.

- ➤ People who have a lot of self-confidence focus on what their strengths are, not on what they cannot do.

- ➤ Physical fitness has a huge effect on self-confidence. If you're out of shape, you will feel insecure, unattractive, and less energetic.

- ➤ Keep growing. Self-confidence rises and falls depending on what you are doing with yourself. If you happen to slack off and choose not to keep improving, you will begin to feel uninspired and less confident.

- ➤ Eliminate self-criticism and continue to speak life into yourself.

Prayer

Dear Heavenly Father,

My desire is to be the woman you created me to be. Help me to appreciate and love every part of me. Help me to not compare myself to other women and covet the special gifts in other women. Help me to understand that other women are beautiful, but I am what my husband wants. Help me to understand that no other person on earth is like me. I have special gifts and a wonderful personality that no one else has. God, help me to take care of my body, and continue to develop and grow as a woman. I want to be happy in my own skin and I always want to be attractive to my husband. Guide me and order my steps. Help me to never become stagnant in any area of my life. Help me to see and appreciate the treasures within me. I want to fall in love with myself. I don't want to be a boring wife. I'm ready to have fun with my husband again. I pray that I will gain confidence in myself. I'm ready to go to another level. Thank you for giving me a new level of confidence and security in myself and an appreciation for what I have to offer. In Jesus name I pray, Amen.

6

Don't Talk About It. Pray About It.

Have you ever known someone who complains about what's going wrong in their life every time you see them? It seems as if their life is based around telling the same stories. They never change because they hide behind their problems. That is what happens when we don't give our problems to God. Sometimes we can get so caught up talking about our mountains that we fail to speak to our mountains. Prayer is an ingredient that should not be excluded from your marriage. Prayer is the glue that will hold it all together when everything is coming against your marriage. It does not matter if your marriage has been on life support for years. Praying over your marriage, speaking to your mountains, and walking the Word is what is going to turn it all around. If your problems are worth talking about to other people, they are worth praying about to God. What is concerning you about your husband and your marriage? Don't let your frustration get the best of you. While you and your spouse's own efforts to change may fail, God will change your marriage if you pray.

Prayer has the power to accomplish what nothing else can. Take it to God. Your marriage has the potential to bless both you and your spouse in significant ways. So don't settle for less than the best in your marriage. Go after the best God has for you and your spouse by praying for your marriage. When you go to God concerning your marriage, be specific about what you need Him to do for you. Psalm 55:22 says, *"Cast your cares on the LORD and He will sustain you; he will never let the righteous fall."* It doesn't matter what it looks like. The scripture says to cast your cares on the Lord and He will keep you from going under.

Before you do anything, make sure that your marriage is built on the Word of God. Even if you are the only saved one in the house, there has to be someone who is sending up prayers to God and worshipping God in the home. If your marriage is built on anything but the Word of God, it will not stand when the storms come. Luke 6:46-49 talks about the wise and foolish builders of a house. Check it out:

Why do you call me, 'Lord, Lord,' and do not do what I say? I will show you what he is like who comes to me and hears my words and puts them into practice. He is like a man building a house, which dug down deep and laid the foundation on rock. When a flood came, the torrent struck that house but could not shake it, because it was well built. But the one who hears my words and does not put them into practice is like a man who built a house on the ground without a foundation. The moment the torrent struck that house, it collapsed and its destruction was complete." Luke 6:46-49

You cannot treat your spouse any kind of way and live any kind of way and not think that the marriage won't crumble. Jesus said they were quick to call him 'Lord, Lord' when the storm came. But before the storm, they were not putting His word into practice. You cannot disrespect your husband, deny him sex, and let yourself go and expect a 'Lord,

Lord' prayer to fix it overnight. So, make sure that the Word of God is the foundation your marriage stands on so that when the floods come against it, it can stand. Make your relationship with Jesus your main concern over your marriage and encourage your husband to do the same. If you both make Jesus your first love, His love will fill your marriage and empower you to love each other more. Be sure to look to God, not your spouse, for your security and self-esteem. Don't expect your spouse to do what only God can do for you. Pray for both you and your spouse to have the wisdom and power to rely on God every day rather than putting unnecessary strain on each other. Prayer must be the foundation for everything that you do. I want to let you know that you cannot change your husband; only God can. Your job is to accept your husband as he is and pray for God to work in his life. Only God can bring about changes that will last. So do not go to family and friends telling all your business and talking down on your husband. Go to God often confessing your need to be changed and invite God to continue His good work in your life.

Emotional Intimacy and Open Communication

Emotional intimacy occurs in marriage when the trust level and communication between two people is such that it fosters the mutual sharing of each other's innermost selves. There are so many different situations that could come up in a marriage to make a spouse feel emotionally neglected. I don't know what your situation is but make sure you take it to God in prayer. There are so many small foxes that hinder emotional intimacy in a marriage. You have bitterness in a spouse, not putting a spouse first, stubbornness, anger, addictions, depression, financial problems and more. Lack of emotional intimacy is one of the main causes for women having affairs. If a man can get us emotionally, he can get us sexually. If you do not guard your heart and spirit, it will be easy to fall prey to the attention of another man. I have seen it happen so many times. Prayer is so important because your spouse cannot meet all your needs. The only one who can meet all your needs is God. The bible says,"*In God's presence there is a fullness of joy.*" If seeking God is not a habit for you now, I beseech you to add it to your daily "to do" list. It is imperative that you go to God concerning the emotional connection between you and your spouse. If you are lacking emotional intimacy in your marriage, do not add fuel to the fire. It is the flesh's nature to want to punish your husband for not being there for you at a time when you really need him. Do not drag out issues by ignoring him, outright denying him, giving silent treatment, or holding grudges. This only creates resentment and further emotional distance. Be emotionally present and prepared to share your true feelings. Encourage your partner to do the same by listening well, and accepting and understanding his truth (though it might not be the same as yours) when he does open up to you. It is important that you are there for your husband without judging him. Express your appreciation for your partner with simple, kind gestures.

When there is conflict going on in your marriage, someone has to be the mature one. Strive to make open communication a routine. Strive to set aside time for each other with no television or computer as distractions. Small acts of affection can mean the world, and are one of the easiest ways to build strong emotional bonds. The last thing you need is two people walking around with negative energy. When your husband is withdrawing from you emotionally, you need to see the bigger picture and get on your face before God. Pray over your husband and ask God to meet him at his point of need. The Bible describes the marriage of a man and a woman as a visual example of the spiritual union between Jesus Christ and the church (all Christians). There is someone who wants to destroy that living example and his name is Satan. John 10:10 says, "*The thief (Satan) comes only to steal, kill, and destroy.*" He desires to destroy marriages.

So many times we fail to see the real enemy in our marital struggles. Ephesians 6:12 says, "*For our struggle is not against flesh and blood, but against rulers, against the authorities, against the powers of darkness, and against the spiritual forces of evil in the heavenly realms.*" There have been times when I would let an argument go on for days with my husband. I would walk around full of pride. Giving my husband the cold shoulder was not a problem for me. I was trying to make him pay for whatever I felt he was not giving me. Those are not the characteristics of a godly wife and that is not the way to handle things. I had to stop and ask myself, "*Who is the real enemy here?*" There is a spiritual battle going on around us that we cannot even see, and it is a greater reality than what our five senses can detect. It is an attack to kill, steal, and destroy the bond between a husband and a wife. Cover your marriage in prayer concerning the emotional intimacy, recognize Satan is the true enemy, and be the wife that your husband needs and watch God turn it all around.

Sexual Intimacy

I really just want to touch on this subject briefly and will elaborate on it more in the next chapter. Let me say this though. If you are single and reading this, if you are selfish and do not feel you should have to have sex with your husband if you don't feel like it, then you need to stay single.

Now for the matters you wrote about: It is good for a man not to marry. But since there is so much immorality, each man should have his own wife and each woman her own husband. The husband should fulfill his marital duty to his wife, and likewise the wife to her husband. The wife's body does not belong to her alone but also to her husband. In the same way, the husband's body does not belong to him alone but also to his wife. Do not deprive each other except by mutual consent and for a time, so that you may devote yourselves to prayer. Then come together again so that Satan will not tempt you because of your lack of self-control. 1 Corinthians 7:1-5

It would surprise you to know how many wives do not actually realize the importance of sexual intimacy in their marriage. They withhold themselves not knowing the damage and rejection it causes in a husband. This passage specifically says that once you got married, your body no longer belongs to you. It belongs to your husband. Verse 5 clearly states that you are not to deprive each other sexually. Wives, listen. When you don't meet your husband's sexual needs, you tempt him to get those needs met elsewhere. I am not saying that your husband is excused to cheat because of it but you sure are not helping the situation. In this passage, the bible discusses a spouse going on a fast. It instructs you to come on back and make love to your spouse once you come off this fast, lest you be tempted for lack of self-control. This thing is serious.

You might be reading this thinking about what your husband needs to do. But this book is to help you focus on what you need to do as a wife. This book is to help you make deposits into your marriage account that will bless you tremendously. It is a bad feeling going to the bank and finding that what you thought was in the account is not there. You want to have something to withdraw when it is time. Ask God to protect you and your spouse's sexual relationship. Pray for the ability to always put each other first instead of hurting each other through selfish decisions. Ask God to send His Spirit to empower you to overcome lust and anything else that can draw your hearts away from each other. Pray for the strength you need to avoid temptations. Ask God to reveal every secret sin in your lives so you each can confess and repent. Learn to live in a way that pleases God. Ask God to help you pay attention to your spouse's needs and desires, and fulfill your spouse sexually. Pray that you will always be attracted to one another and faithful in both thought and deed.

Oneness in Finances

You cannot have a great relationship until you can communicate and agree about money. Money is either the best or the worst area of communication in our marriages. One of the main reasons for conflict is that, as husband and wives, we come from different backgrounds. Sometimes we share a common view of how to handle money, but more often our perspectives set us apart from one another. It is hard to see how a couple could divorce over money until you get in a situation where a spouse loses his or her job and the stress starts kicking in. You start fighting, bills start getting behind, bill collectors are calling and the wife is getting stressed and putting pressure on the husband. Thoughts of doing anything for quick money start rolling through your mind. It gets crazy sometimes. I was born in the hood. I learned how to survive when tough times hit. When you were not raised in struggle, it is hard to adapt to living in it. I have been there. I know how it feels to have to eat Ramen Noodles more than one night and having to borrow money from people to make it. It's no fun.

When you and your husband are not able to come to some type of medium in the marriage, there is going to be trouble. Disagreeing about money is not the problem; it's how you work through your disagreements and differences so you both eventually become satisfied with the outcome. We spend years shaping and honing our individual viewpoints, watching the monetary habits of our parents, friends, and mentors. So it is important to learn to work as a team when it comes to finances. I have seen people divorce over money because money was hidden by one spouse and the other didn't know about it. Spouses started opening secret accounts. Spouses didn't want to work with a budget. And I have seen them divorce because there was no control and just too much shopping. It's bad when a marriage has no unity concerning finances. If you and your husband are having problems agreeing with the finances, I suggest you take time to discuss and thoroughly understand your income, insurance plans, investments, and assets as a couple. Always try to understand where your spouse is coming from in fights concerning finances. Don't worry if you must agree to disagree. As longs as everyone is okay with the final outcome, do what works best for both of you. Make it a habit of praying about your finances. Remember that it is God who has given you the ability to earn money, and everything ultimately belongs to Him. Ask God to give you and your spouse the wisdom and discipline to manage money well. Pray for the help you need to work diligently to earn money. Give generously to support God's work on earth, avoid foolish spending decisions and debt, and save consistently.

You might not always want to pray for your spouse when you're angry. But that is when you really should pray...when it is the hardest. Prayer does not always change things for you. Sometimes you need to change more than your circumstances. Your spouse is not your enemy. James 5:16 says, *"Confess your sins to each other and pray for each other so that you may be healed. The earnest prayer of a righteous person has great power and produces wonderful results."* Sis, there is NOTHING too hard for our God. Trust in His Word. Believe that your prayers are powerful and are producing great results in your marriage. Don't give up. Sometimes you have to suffer and go through painful experiences within your marriage. But know that the road to "for better" sometimes has to go through "for worse." Don't breakdown before your breakthrough.

Points To Remember

- Don't go around spreading your business to your family/friends about your husband and what is going on in your marriage. If it is a matter of abuse or something very serious, that's another story. Or if the two of you cannot handle a serious problem together, you might want to seek counseling. Otherwise, take your cares to God and pray about it.

- Don't tear your marriage down with your own hands and then call on God for a quick fix only for you to continue mistreating your husband. Build the marriage up and cover it in prayer.

- Know that your husband is not the real enemy. The real enemy is Satan and his desire is to kill, steal, and destroy your marriage.

- Pray that the emotional intimacy in your marriage will be very strong and rewarding for you and your husband. Pray that both of you will both be emotionally fulfilled and never stop loving your spouse even when he is not doing his part. He cannot meet all your needs. Only God can.

- Pray that you and your husband will satisfy each other sexually and that nothing will come between you.

- Pray that you and your husband will be good stewards over your finances and work as a team concerning your money.

Shei Atkins

Prayer

(Confession)

Dear Heavenly Father,

I come to you covering my husband and my marriage in prayer. I take authority over my marriage in Jesus name and release your power to work in both of our lives. I am willing to see my errors and work on myself, no matter how I've been offended by what my spouse has done. I ask you to help me see the truth about myself. I know that you can resurrect my marriage. I humble myself and repent my part in making it unhealthy. (Be specific about what you've done and confess it). Help me and my husband to always trust each other enough to share our thoughts and feelings openly and honestly with each other. Teach me how to communicate well with my husband. Help us speak positive words that encourage each other and help us to avoid speaking negative words that tear each other down. Show us how to listen to each other well. I'm asking you for the wisdom to speak the right words at the right time. I cancel Satan's plan to cause strife in my marriage through miscommunication. God, help us both settle conflict in healthy, productive, and loving ways. Bring my husband and me into unity with each other. Free us from the effects of negative emotions that have influenced our marriage. Deliver us from all negative attitudes that we have allowed to control or damage our lives. I ask for a release of your healing in our marriage. Continue to work in our lives. I look beyond my current circumstances and place all of my hope in you.

(Good Parents)

Father, I ask you to give us wisdom about how best to raise our children. Lord, allow us to see what we need to see about ourselves and each child. Strengthen us to keep our parental duties in the right balance so we can focus well on our children without neglecting our marriage relationship. I pray for the ability to keep our marriage top priority, no matter how busy we are with the children. I put our family into your hands and trust you with every aspect of their lives.

(Meet Each Others Needs)

God, help us to see eye-to-eye about financial decisions. I put my trust in you rather than in money because I know that when I trust in you, everything will be okay no matter what our current situation. Protect my husband and me from any kind of self-destructive behavior. Open our eyes to see if we've allowed any habits into our lives that have the potential to harm us – and if so, free us from their grip. I take all our concerns to you in prayer instead of looking to other sources that will only give me temporary comfort and harm me in the process. Help us to be completely honest with each other and not secretly hide things from each other. Give me ears to hear my spouse without resentment if he confronts me about a problem. Strengthen me to resist temptation. Restore all the damage that has occurred in our lives so that we can enjoy the abundant life together that you intend for us to have.

(Sexual Intimacy)

Protect me and my husband's sexual relationship. I pray for the ability to always put each other first instead of hurting each other through selfish decisions. Send your Spirit to empower us to overcome lust and anything else that can draw our hearts away from each other. I pray for the strength I need to avoid temptations. Reveal every hidden sin in our lives so we each can confess and repent. Teach me to live in a way that pleases you. Help me pay attention to your husband's needs and desires, and fulfill him sexually. I pray that we'll always be attracted to one another and faithful in both thought and action.

(Hardened Hearts)

Keep our marriage from the damage caused by stubborn or disobedient hearts. I confess any pride or stubbornness I've had toward you or my husband. Transform our hearts so that we'll always feel love for each other. Give me a clean heart so I'll naturally want to please you. I trust you to restore my marriage.

(Priorities)

God, help me to always keep my relationship with you my top priority and my relationship with my husband next under that. Help my husband and me to be able to choose each other over everything else that tries to distract us. I need your help to make the necessary changes in my schedule to give my husband the time he needs and constantly nurture my marriage.

(Divorce)

God, help my husband and me rise above thinking of divorce as a solution to our problems. I repent of any time I've threatened my husband with divorce or even thought about it. I pray for the possibility of divorce never to enter our minds. Give us strength to focus on building up our marriage instead of tearing it down.

(Infidelity)

I confess any thoughts or actions of infidelity. Protect my marriage from infidelity and give my husband and me the wisdom and strength to avoid temptations that can harm our relationship. Help us forgive each other and rebuild trust back in our relationship. Create in me a clean heart and renew the right spirit within me. Change my heart so that my sexual desire would be only toward my husband.

(Separation)

Father, keep my husband and me closely connected to each other and help us to avoid neglect. Nothing can ever separate me from your love. I rely on that love to allow me to grow closer to my husband. Pour out your love and draw my husband and me closer together. Help us to be kind when we could be sarcastic, merciful when we could be judgmental and forgiving when we could take offense. Protect us from the small foxes that destroy relationships. Let there be full reconciliation in my marriage.

(Miraculous Power)

Heavenly Father, I give my marriage to you and place my hope in you and trust in your unfailing love. I focus on you rather than on my circumstances. Your Word says that you will never leave or forsake me. My marriage has been on life support for some time. I ask you to resurrect it, no matter how dead it seems. You have the power to do it and I know that you want the best for both my husband and me. I pray that we will grow even stronger in faith, in you, and in each other.

7

Keeping Your Man Interested In You Only

If you want your marriage to come out tasting the same, you need to cook it the same way you've been cooking it. Do what works. You cannot leave out any ingredients. This is usually where a lot of marriages start to go downhill. The same thing it took to get your baby hooked is the same thing it will take to keep him. You cannot stop doing what you did to get your man and think that it will not affect the relationship. You do want your man to stay interested in you only, right? Okay, well you've got to step your game up. Do you know that there are ladies out there waiting on you to mess up? Ladies hit on our men all the time, we just don't know about them all. You want to make sure your man is satisfied when he leaves the house. Have you ever been starving while watching television and a pizza commercial or Red Lobster commercial came on that made you want some? I know I have. Have you noticed that when you are full, you could care less about eating? Even though the food on the commercial looked good, you didn't want it. Why? Because you were satisfied. The same thing applies to your man.

When you are taking care of your man sexually, emotionally, and mentally stimulating him, it does not matter how good she looks because he's satisfied. It is when you stop doing the things you know he likes that those commercials start tempting him. The lady on the job who has been complimenting him starts getting his attention now. He now starts noticing the ladies dressing sexy while his wife is walking around in big holey pajama pants and a raggedy t-shirt. All men may be different as far as what they look for in a woman and what type of women they like. But one thing all these men will have in common is that they each want their woman to keep doing what she did to hook him in. If you are not treating your husband right and your man is still treating you right, you need to stop and give God praise right now. You've got yourself a good man.

You should not be surprised if your man starts looking elsewhere if you haven't been giving him what he needs. Never get comfortable in your wifey position. Remember I told you there are women out there who are ready and willing to do what you won't do. The minute you start slipping up is the minute you open the door for the enemy to come into your marriage. You know you can open the door to the enemy, right? Hopefully, you have a good man who loves God and has self-control. But no matter how much God a man has in him, you need to know that your man is human and there is only so long you can neglect his needs without him getting tempted to go elsewhere. Let Mama Shei give you a few tips on how to keep your man interested in you.

Keep It Sexy

I don't care how spiritual you are. Your man wants you to turn off the tongues and turn him on. Turn off the television and turn on your man. You know those little things you did when you knew he was coming over or you were going out back when you first started dating What did you do? You made sure you looked good. You made sure you smelled great. You made sure you were clean, just in case. You made sure your hair was looking good. What happened to that lady? Your husband married you because everything you did was what he wanted in a woman. He saw himself spending the rest of his life with you and therefore, proposed to you. You kept it sexy and you made sure you were pleasing to his eye. If you've been slipping in keeping is sexy for your man, I need you to find that lady and bring her back quickly! Your husband deserves it. You deserve it! If you've been slipping in the lingerie area, it's time to go shopping. Hair all over the head and grandma panties are not cute. Men like to show their women off in public, too. The bible says when a man finds a wife, he finds a good thing. We are like their trophies. They feel good when everyone sees their good thing on their arm. The bible says love never fails and is not conditional. But part of loving your husband is keeping yourself up and not letting yourself go.

You know what your husband likes. Get back to it. Even if you have gained a few pounds and are overweight, you can still keep it sexy. If your man isn't attracted to you any longer because of the weight gain, do what it takes to make him happy. You may have to drop your pride in order to do it, but it's all about keeping your man's attention. Have you thought about the fact that you are the ONLY woman your husband is legally allowed to sleep with for the rest of your lives together? Men are visual and you have to do what it takes these days. You have to stay on your game, girl. You know what your husband likes sexually. Take care of your man! If he likes kissing, kiss him. If he likes you to initiate sex, do it. If he didn't initiate sex, would you ever have it? Initiate, girl! Make time to please your man and give him what he wants. It will take your marriage to a whole new level. When you let yourself go, you are really taking your husband for granted and saying to yourself, "It doesn't matter what I do. He married me and he's going to be right here." Your heart might not feel that way, but that is what your actions are saying. You have seen the divorces and affairs occurring out here. They all made the same vows and promises that you made. I don't think anybody goes into marriage with intentions on divorcing. But something happens along the way. They stop putting each other first. Go back to putting your man first. Girlfriend, get you a sexy dress to wear when you go out with your husband. Get a nice pair of jeans and a top to accent your shape and go back to doing what you did when you were dating. Keeping it sexy will keep your husband bragging about you and keep him interested in you only.

Cooking For Your Man

This section might not apply to every woman because I know that all women do not cook and some men cook for their women. But this section is for the ladies who know they spoiled their man with that good cooking in the beginning and have been slacking. Even if you aren't slacking, you know what your man likes. Cooking for your man is a form of serving your man. Men love to be catered to and treated like kings. If you want to be treated like a queen, treat your man like a king. There is nothing like coming home to a nicely cooked meal after a long day's work. Cooking for your man shows that you love him and desire to keep him happy. Even if you are not getting along, you should still be mature about it and continue to serve him. He won't stay mad too long after that. There have been times my husband and I weren't getting along and we still cooked for each other. It's sort of like an icebreaker. It shows that even though you're upset, you are still going to love each other through it. So if you know your man loves his woman to cook for him, keep him interested in you by satisfying him with a good home-cooked meal.

Encourage and Support You Man

Proverbs 31:16 says that the virtuous wife speaks with wisdom and instruction is on her tongue. Encouragement and support are where a lot of women fall short. If you are married, your man should love talking to you. He should be happy to come home and hate to leave because being in your presence is just that awesome. There are many reasons why a man would shut down on you. Lack of encouragement and lack of support at home will surely do it. Ladies, you do not want it to get to that point. If your husband has turned to shut-down mode, make it a point to let him know that you are there for him. He needs to feel confident that he can talk to his wife. Proverbs 18:21 says, *"Death and life are in the power of the tongue; those who make it a friend shall eat its fruit."* That means that you need to be mindful of the things you say to your husband. You are either speaking life or death into your husband. To encourage means to give courage or confidence to or raise the hopes. The way to encourage your husband is by the words you speak. The world is full of people to discourage you with their words. Words are powerful. God used words to speak the world into existence. Out of everything God created, He blessed man with the gift of words. We have a choice to use our words for good or evil. Our men love admiration and our support. They also love a woman who is a good listener. Women love to talk. Don't be so busy trying to prove your point that you fail to hear your husband's heart. When you know your husband's heart, you can be the support that he needs without judgment. Life gets very tough for a man. There is pressure with work and just pressure to please and to try to live up to the expectations of everybody. He plays different roles in his life. To one, he's a father; to another, a son; to you, a husband; an employee on the job, plus more. Everyone is expecting something from him. Then he has the pressure to take care of his household and make sure his wife is happy. You as his wife should be the one to take the load off of him, not add to his troubles. If you have a man that is trying to make it work with you and you are in shut-down mode, you are making a big mistake. There are so many women who long to have a man who is willing to communicate with them. Never take advantage of your husband just because you have been married for ten years or more. Being married ten years doesn't guarantee an eleventh year. You can walk around for so long holding grudges before it backfires. When the effort to make the marriage work on both ends stops, you are looking at a tragedy. Your man will shut down on you and avoid sharing things with you when you are not supportive.

If you have something negative to say every time he tries to talk to you, he feels rejected and will eventually end up not talking to you at all. If you tear him down using words like "You never", "You're always", and other sarcastic things, if won't be long before he puts a guard over his heart. Men hate sarcasm. They hate when we make smart comments that sting like bullets when we're angry. They hate when we ignore them when they ask us questions. Is it easy for your husband to talk to you? If not, you need to make some quick changes and become the wife that he needs. Why is it so hard for your husband to talk to you? What is so hard about opening up to your man? When you fail to communicate with your man, your actions are telling him that you do not want the marriage. Is that what you want?

When everyone tells your husband he can't, he needs to hear from you that he can. When he feels like he cannot make it, you need to be the one who tells him that he can. Your husband needs you just as much as you need him. You should be your husband's number one fan. Men need encouraging words from the women in their lives, starting with mama, continuing on with sisters and cousins, and hopefully ending with their wives. They never outgrow the need for encouragement whether they are five years old or 70 years old. It is a wife's job to make her home a place of peace, rest, and comfort to give her husband a break from the burdens he deals with outside the home. You also need to be in tune with your husband's feelings of accomplishment and failures, hopes and aspirations, doubts and concerns, pleasures and disappointments, and his vulnerabilities. Make your home a safe haven from the pressures of life by building your husband up with encouraging words, and supporting him in his endeavors. That will make him one happy man. Never use your words to tear down your husband. There are plenty of women out there who will encourage him, let him know how sexy he looks, and compliment him. When you fail to support and encourage your man, you make it very easy for another woman to fill that void in his life. You do not want that. That is how emotional affairs start. So, keep your man interested in you by adoring, admiring, and appreciating him with words that build up instead of words that destroy.

Trustworthy

If you do not have trust in your recipe for love, your marriage will be bitter to the taste. We as women always talk about how men cheat and are no good. Truth be told, women cut up just as much as men do. I have seen so many women cheating on their husbands that it doesn't make any sense. Trust is a part of the glue that holds a relationship together. If you do not have trust in your relationship, you are headed for trouble. Can your husband trust you? Proverbs 31 describe the qualities of a virtuous woman, and being trustworthy is one of them. Proverbs 31:10-12 says, *"An excellent wife who can find? For her worth is far above jewels. The heart of her husband trusts in her, And he will have no lack of gain. She does him good and not evil all the days of her life."*

You need to continue to walk in the character of Christ if you want your husband to keep his focus on you alone. It turns a man off when a woman is disrespectful, mouthy, and manipulative. A quick way to turn your man's heart away from you is to start lying and being dishonest. You have to be honest about the money, honest about your feelings, and pure in your heart. Here in proverbs, it says the heart of her husband trusts in her and she does him good and not evil all the days of her life. That means that there are some evil women out there who do not have their husbands' best interests at heart. We as women are very emotional and I have seen many women cheat who weren't getting their emotional needs met at one time. Can your husband trust you to be faithful even when he does not love you the way he should at times? Can he trust you to be faithful when he goes out of town for a few days? Can your husband trust you to be a faithful and respectful woman around attractive gentlemen you work with or encounter at church?

Let's keep it real. Women long to feel beautiful. After being married a few years and having a baby or two, sometimes some of us wonder if we still have it. Then some fine man that you work with or see at your favorite store comes along and gives you a compliment and your heart starts to jump. That is normal. But if that compliment or attention you get from another man starts taking your mind somewhere it doesn't need to be and has you craving for more attention from that man, you need to flee! That is how we get caught up. The best way to prevent that kind of temptation is to ignore it. Men try to talk to me all the time, but I don't entertain it. Those men are not worth my marriage. It does not matter how good a man looks or how much money he makes, he is not worth your marriage.

The enemy will show you the pleasure you will get out of the situation. The enemy will show you everything your husband isn't doing. He

NEVER shows you how heartbroken your husband will be. He NEVER shows you the embarrassment you are going to have facing all the people you let down who admired and respected you. He does not show you how your children are watching you and learning those same behaviors. Flee temptation, sister girl! God has given you a way of escape. Can your husband trust you to handle the finances properly? Can he trust you to love him even through the rough times? Can he trust you to love him the same if the marriage hits a rough spot and he loses his job or car? If you are showing signs that you cannot be trusted, your husband will lose his interest in you. His perception of you will change and the way he views you will change. You never want it to get to that point. Be the trustworthy wife that your husband longs for. Be the trustworthy wife your husband isn't ashamed of. Keep or gain your husband's interest and attention by continuing or striving to be the godly woman that he desires and is attracted to.

Points To Remember

- When you stop doing what you did to hook your man in the beginning, your relationship will start going downhill.

- What you won't do for your man, another woman will and is ready to do it.

- When your husband is satisfied at home, it is easier to resist outside temptations.

- When your husband is not satisfied at home, it makes outside temptation so much harder to resist.

> The minute you start slipping is the minute you open the door for the enemy to come into your marriage.

> If you want your man to be interested in you only, you must continually keep it sexy for him, take care of his wants and desires, encourage and support him, and he must be confident in knowing that he can trust you concerning the money, faithfulness, with his feelings, his heart, and protecting his image.

Prayer

Dear Heavenly Father,

I thank you for who you are in my life. I realize that by neglecting my husband and marriage, I can open up the door for the enemy to come in. Help me to always do the things my husband likes and do them well. Help me to please him sexually, emotionally, and mentally stimulate him. I cannot take care of his spiritual needs so I ask you to minister to him spiritually and fill any voids that I cannot fill. Help me continue to attract his eye by keeping myself up. Help me to maintain a sex appeal that my husband cannot resist. I ask that you give me the wisdom on how to make and keep my home a safe haven for my husband to come to. I release your peace, joy, and comfort into our home. I pray that I will not become the nagging wife who is annoying like a constant dripping faucet. Let the words that come out of my mouth build up and edify my husband up. Keep me from speaking death into my husband and may I never be the cause of his discouragement, but the gain of his confidence. Help me to always encourage, uplift, admire, and respect my husband. Keep me from betraying his trust. Help me to show my husband that I have his back and that I'm his number one fan. Help me to remain faithful in meeting my husband's needs, in my love and support for him, and in respecting him. In Jesus name, Amen.

8

Stroking Your Man's Ego

Have you ever eaten a meal and knew there was something in this recipe that just put the icing on the cake, but you couldn't quite put your finger on what it was? I'm talking about one of those secret recipes that have been passed down through the generations. Well, if you want your love recipe to be off the chain, you might want to learn how to stroke your man's ego. There are a few different definitions of ego. One definition is an exaggerated sense of self-importance or conceit. That is not the ego I'm talking about. The ego I am referring to is appropriate pride in oneself or self-esteem. Remember, I told you about speaking life into your man. Well stroking your man's ego is all about speaking life into your man in a way that will have him walking like George Jefferson. Do you want to have your man eating out of the palm of your hand? Stroke his ego. Do you want to be on your man's mind all day? Stroke his ego. Do you want to make your man feel appreciated to the tenth power? Stroke his ego. Men like to feel needed and want to hear that all their efforts are not going to waste. When you see and hear about men cheating, you better believe that there are some sisters out there stroking those brothers' egos. When you stroke your man's ego, you will have him coming back for more and more. When he does not feel needed, you better believe he is going to gravitate the other way. When a man leaves a relationship, you better know that he gravitated toward some woman who was stroking his ego and making him feel like the king of all kings. I am not saying that this is right, but I am trying to show you how to keep your man and keep him close. Stroke his ego.

To stroke your man's ego, you need to let him know how happy he makes you. Even if he doesn't succeed at trying to please you, do not belittle him. Acknowledge his effort and let him know you appreciate his effort. A lot of women have a hard time understanding how a man could leave a woman most people would consider a ten and end up with what society would call a six. Good looks are cool, but good looks alone won't keep a man at home. You have to do more than sit and look cute. A sister who may not be what you call a head turner can still turn a man's heart by stroking his ego. Have you ever seen a good looking guy walking with a woman and wondered how she got him? Trust and believe, she was stroking his ego. Men are sensitive beings who require as much validation and connection as women. You have to learn how to make your man feel like he is the best thing since sliced bread. Men are experts at picking up a woman's vibe and body language. So send off the body language that lets a man know that you are approachable if you're single and ready for love.

Compliments and Attention

One way to stroke your man's ego is to give him your undivided attention when listening to him. I have been guilty of typing on the computer or watching television while my husband tried to talk to me. That is more disrespectful than anything. It shows lack of interest and slight rejection.

A man will usually ask you if you are listening or smack his lips and walk off. I learned not to do that anymore and I learned the importance of listening to my man. Never give someone else more attention than you give your husband. He won't be too happy about that. I have been guilty of this many times. It could be a family member or even someone who calls your phone. If you are more kind and attentive to other people than you are to your man, it is going to cause some problems. If you really want your marriage, you will do what it takes to please your man. If not, you are heading toward becoming another statistic. So now when my husband is talking to me, I stop what I'm doing and show interest in what he is saying. Everything your husband talks about might not interest you, but stroking his ego is making him feel like he's Barack Obama giving his first speech after the inauguration. Another way to give your man attention is to take notice in him. A woman who pays attention to her man notices when he has gotten a haircut, a facial trim, or a new pair of pants or shirt. Complimenting your man and letting him know how nice his outfit or fresh haircut looks will definitely do the trick.

If you really want to stroke your man's ego, let him know how good he is in bed or how well he pleases you in the bedroom. Be interested in sex. Men love sex - period. If you don't give your man enough sex, he may look elsewhere. If he's a good man, he'll work with you and hang on as long as he can because he loves you. Let your man know that he can have you when he wants by giving him that eye contact every once in a while to show him that you desire him. Variety is also important. Role playing will even spice it up, too. Be spontaneous with the sex. Scheduling your lovemaking sessions is cool to do a couple of times, but it will eventually bore him to death. You can also do more than just have sex to keep his interest. Touching and rubbing him lovingly throughout the day will hook him in, too. Also, when you're making love, don't just lay there like an old mat in a gym. Talk to your man. Let him know how good it feels when he touches you here or there. If you don't talk, then at least let your body language do the talking for you. If your man doesn't sexually please you, do not kill the mood and his ego by letting him know you don't like it while he's trying to please you. Tell him what he can do better at a later time. If he's giving you foreplay that just is not hitting the spot, take control in the situation and please him instead. That will get you heated up. A lot of women don't take enough initiative in the bedroom. If your man stopped doing all the initiating, would you ever have sex? So stroke your man's ego by letting him know how good he is in bed or how he is a good kisser. Give your man attention by initiating sex for a change. Initiating sex lets your man know that he is wanted and desired by you.

Appreciation

Men love to feel appreciated. You can either crush a man's ego or build it up by how you treat him. Your man wants to know that his efforts are appreciated and that they make a difference. He might not have a million dollars in the bank or own a big business, but that shouldn't stop you from making him feel like he does. If your man doesn't make a lot of money, let him know how much you appreciate him taking care of the family. Go into detail and let him know how impressed you are with his abilities. Let him know how smart you think he is. You affirming what he does for a living is a great stroke to his ego. Never let another woman tell him how great he is; that is your job. Stroke his mind, girl. Let him know how much you appreciate him taking out the trash. Let him know how great of a job he's doing around the house. What do you admire about him? Tell him how much you admire the wonderful things he does.

Get a Man, Keep a Man

One thing I like about my husband is that he has the ability to take nothing and turn it into something. He is so creative and neat. He can fix a plate and make you feel you're at a high-priced restaurant. He can take something that somebody else threw away and if they see him with it, they would want it back. That is his gift. He can take a person who can't sing and make them sound like they have been singing for years. I notice how he smiles every time I tell him how creative he is and how I wish I could do what he does. It is the simple things that go a long way. In relationships, no one is perfect. We all make mistakes. There will be times in your relationship or marriage that you will hurt your man's feelings. A lot of times pride keeps people from apologizing to each other when they know deep down inside they really wish someone would give in. No man who really cares for his wife is happy walking around giving her the cold shoulder. When you and your man aren't talking, a sincere apology will melt his anger away. Saying you're sorry is like offering to carry heavy bags for a woman. It takes a load off and it brings such relief to your man. Letting your man know that you were wrong and how sorry you are actually strokes his ego. It shows him how much you care about him and that you want to be close to him. It will definitely make him smile. On the other hand, if you find yourself having to apologize too much, then eventually your apologies won't mean a thing. But making up with your man can be a very special event. It shows maturity in you and shows your man that you really want to make this thing work. I don't know if you have ever read Song of Solomon in the bible. If not, that would be great read for you. It will definitely show you how to stroke a man's ego. Song of Solomon 1:16 says, *"How handsome you are, my lover! Oh how charming! And our bed is luxuriant."* That book of the bible is a must read for anyone who needs an example of how to romance, admire, and stroke their spouse's ego. Remember, what you won't do, another woman will. So, take care of your man.

Points To Remember

- Make it your purpose to constantly have your man walking like George Jefferson by building his self-esteem with encouraging words.

- Men like to feel needed and want to hear that all their efforts aren't going to waste.

- The only edge of a man's other woman is that she knows how to stroke a man's ego. Give your man what he needs so he does not look for it elsewhere.

- Even if your man does not succeed at trying to please you, do not belittle him. Acknowledge his effort and let him know you appreciate him trying.

- Stroke your man's ego by giving him your undivided attention when he is talking.

- Stroke your man's ego by acknowledging his efforts in the home and letting him know that he is appreciated and makes a difference.

- Stroke your man's ego by telling him how good he is in bed or showing him through your body language.

- Stroke your man's ego by sucking up to him through an apology when you're wrong.

- Song of Solomon is a great bible read and is a great example of how to stroke your man's ego using the power of words.

Prayer

Dear Heavenly Father,

Thank you for my husband. I recognize that the same way you like your children to praise you, my husband loves it the same. Help me become my husband's number one fan. Let my words speak life into him on a continual basis. Never let me be the cause of his sorrow. When he's down, help me to build him up. Help me to always encourage him and let him know that he is the best. Allow my actions to back up every encouraging word I say to my husband. Use me to build my husband up in all areas of his life. Help me to walk in humility concerning my marriage and be mature enough to apologize to my husband when I'm wrong. I ask that nothing will hinder me from giving my husband the attention that he needs. God keep my husband so that he will not gravitate to get attention from outside sources sent from the enemy. Help me to never allow life destroying words and words of death to enter into our marriage recipe. In Jesus name, Amen.

9

Why Respect Is So Important

Respect is one thing you don't even want to think about excluding out of the recipe for love. Respect is one thing a man cannot live without. Respect is defined as an act of giving particular attention or the state or quality of being esteemed. This is exactly what your man wants from you. He wants you to give particular attention to the things he does and to esteem him at all times. The opposite of respect is disrespect. A sure way to turn your man's heart away from you is to disrespect him. Disrespect is defined as lack of respect, esteem, or courteous regard. In Ephesians 5:33, God commands a woman to respect her husband. It reads, *"Each one of you (men) must love his wife as he loves himself, and the wife must respect her husband."*

Disrespecting your husband can be done without even using words. You can also disrespect your husband in your actions. When your actions go against the very thing your man desires, it is disrespect. When you purposefully do something you know your husband does not like, it is disrespect. It is also disrespectful to a man when you make important decisions without even considering him. How, you ask? Remember, I told you that respect is an act of giving particular attention. For the simple fact that you did not even consider him concerning an important household decision is disrespectful. I believe that God commands women to respect their husbands because He knows that there will be many situations that occur when you do not want to show it. It is hard to respect a man when he is not giving you any attention when he comes home. It is hard to respect a man when he doesn't call and check in when he knows it is important to you as his wife. It is hard to respect a man who puts his job and hobbies before you. It is hard to respect a man who makes a lot of dumb decisions. It is hard to respect a man who won't work or a man who just seems like he's not trying hard enough to find a job while you are busting your butt trying to make ends meet. These are the times when you have to respect him even when your flesh does not want to.

Loving like God loves is treating your husband like he already has the qualities that you like. There is a quote that says, "Don't treat a person how they act. Treat them how you want them to be and watch them become it." What you are doing is planting seeds into your man and speaking those things into existence. That totally goes against what we have been taught. We as women have been taught how a man has to earn our respect in order for us to give respect. That is backwards. Ephesians 5:33 doesn't say, "Wives, respect your husband as long as he does everything right." Respecting and loving your husband should be done regardless of how your husband is treating you. I am not saying you should let a man disrespect and abuse you. What I mean is that it is so easy for us as women to retaliate, point fingers and play the same game we feel our husbands are playing when we are not happy in the marriage. The way you win against the enemy is to do what the Word says. When we as women are angry at our husbands, we tend to yell, nag, belittle and disrespect our husbands. It feels good to the flesh, yet it is ineffective.

Never Disrespect Your Man In Public

The most effective way to make a man feel unloved is to disrespect him, especially in front of others. Ridiculing, dominating, or dismissing your husband in front of someone else is not the way to go if you want to make your husband feel loved. It's bad enough if you do it in private, but in public, you might as well slap him in the face. Ladies, never disrespect your husbands in public or allow anyone else to do it. Sometimes your husband will do things that may embarrass or anger you while you are out somewhere. Be mature about it. It is easy to act a fool. Trust me. Never yell at your man in public places, roll your eyes at him in front of others, or undercut him in front of others. You should never do it privately either. The bible says that a soft answer turns away wrath. Your role is to remain the peacemaker in your home.

You don't overcome evil with evil. You overcome evil with good. Never let family, friends, or anyone else badmouth your husband. Sometimes when people hear you speaking negatively about your husband, they feel like they have a right to do it, too, but then you want to get mad. The best way to handle that is to not even start it. This is something I never do. It is very disrespectful and embarrassing to your man. It also betrays trust. Protect your marriage by keeping people who do not matter out of your business. You cannot run to family and friends every time you and your husband get into an argument and make your man look bad. Do you know what happens when you do that? You change their perception of your husband. Then, when you decide to bring him around again, everyone is looking at your man with the evil eye. Do you feel me? You know better than that. You cannot go to a family member's or friend's house crying and trying to spend the night because of a fight you and your husband had and expect family not to retaliate. You have to learn how to deal with conflict by communicating in a healthy way. Always give your marriage issues to God, and if you two cannot work it out alone, seek counseling from your pastor or someone who can help.

Respect Him By Accepting Him For Who He Is

Do not try to change your spouse. We all have something that we need to work on, and it is each person's own job to figure that out and change it if they want to. You cannot "fix" someone else; you will only make them angry and defensive by trying. It's wrong for a woman to marry a man knowing he is one way and then try to change him to something else after marriage. A lot of times women know what they're getting into and they know the type of man they have. But for some reason, they go into marriage thinking they can change their men. You cannot change your man, and your man cannot change you. God is the only one who does the changing, and a person has to want to change on his or her own first. When you go into marriage, you go in accepting your man the way he is. It's too late to try to change someone once you are tied in. I'm not saying that he can't or won't become better man while you are married. I'm also not saying that you cannot speak the truth in love to him concerning certain issues. Women often make the mistake of wounding their husbands in an attempt to motivate them to change. "You're always doing something stupid!" "Why can't you surprise me and take me out like Stacy's husband? He's much more fun than you. I'm bored with you!" "When are you going bring some real money in this house?" A woman who says hurtful remarks like this assumes that if her "criticisms" are received by her husband, he will change, which will in turn make him a better man. That kind of thinking is farthest from the truth.

Belittling, nagging, and comparing your man to other men will only create anger and frustration inside a man. The result will be a man who is disconnected, bitter, and detached. You will push your husband away from you when you try to change him to fit what you want him to be. Relationships will always have ups and downs. They survive on compromise and being supportive, not yanking a partner's personality around to meet your own. That won't do anything except cause conflict in the marriage. That is where the disrespect begins. When you try to change your man into what you think he should be, you are telling your man that you are not happy with him, and it will show in your actions. Remember, respect is all about esteeming your man and putting him first. There is no way you can respect him when you are trying to change him and constantly nagging him about who and what he isn't. You don't ever want to turn your wife role into a mother role by trying to change him. Really, life is too short. You don't want a boy; you want a man. Successful and happy relationships are built on respect, not the kind when one person in a relationship is convinced that they always know what's best for the other person. Women should not act like that towards their men and men should not act like that toward their women. If you are not married and see some red flags, avoid future problems now by realizing that when it comes to a spouse, what you see is what you get. Do not ignore your man's need for respect. When you disrespect your man by being ungrateful, insulting or humiliating, it will damage him. Don't get me wrong, you can still work on your man without being disrespectful. But you have to be smart about it. In your attempts to change him, be cautious so that it will not come across as disrespect. If you want a man to act another way in your relationship, you are going to have to put insults aside and learn to be respectful. If you treat your husband like a king when he is acting like a frog, he will have to line up and treat you like a queen. It's all about consistently sowing what you want into your marriage and remaining patient, knowing that a harvest takes time to grow. Let me give you a few seeds of love that you can start planting and depositing into your husband.

21 Things You Can Do To Show Love & Respect To Your Husband

1. Thank him for just being himself.

2. Graciously teach him how to demonstrate his love for you.

3. Always respect him in front of the children.

4. Don't criticize him in front of others. Be his number one fan.

5. Express your anger in respectful ways and don't give him the cold shoulder.

6. Always speak the truth in love to him.

7. Praise his good decisions. Diminish the bad ones.

8. Allow him to express himself freely, without fear of you calling him stupid or unreasonable.

9. Initiate and respond to sex more often with your husband.

10. Thank him for things he does around the house. Men really appreciate that.

11. Help your husband to be the spiritual head at home without trying to run him.

12. Respect his desire to do well—not his performance.

13. Admit your mistakes; don't be afraid to be humble. Strip away your pride.

14. Show interest in what he feels is important in life.

15. Try not to make sudden major changes without talking it over with your husband and giving him time to adjust.

16. Purposefully try to understand his feelings—even when you disagree with him.

17. When you go out on a date together don't bring up problems—have fun instead.

18. Give him time to unwind after he gets home from work and set a loving and peaceful atmosphere.

19. Brag about him to other people both in front of him and even when he is not there.

20. Do not give other people more time and attention than you give your spouse. He will notice it and it can cause problems in a marriage.

21. Be his "helpmate" in whatever ways you sense he needs it.

A man needs respect from his wife and this is revealed to him in the way she ministers to him. Your great efforts will not go unnoticed by your husband or by God. Respect your husband at all times and watch it take your marriage to a new level.

Points To Remember

- ➢ Respecting your husband is attending to your husband's needs and ministering to your husband in ways that build his self-esteem. Anything opposite of this is disrespect.

- ➢ Disrespecting your husband is a sure way to turn your husband's heart away from you.

- ➢ In Ephesians 5:33, God commands a wife to respect her husband.

- ➢ When we as women are angry at our husbands, we tend to yell, nag, belittle and disrespect our husbands to try to get them to do what WE want them to do. Doing these things feels good to the flesh, but they are so ineffective.

- ➢ Protect your marriage by keeping people out of your business and relationship.

- ➢ Always overcome a wrong you think your husband has done to you with good.

- ➢ When dating a man, what you see is what you get. Don't marry a man in hopes of trying to change him. You cannot "fix" someone else; you will only make them angry and defensive by trying.

➤ There is no way you can respect your husband when you are trying to change him and you are constantly nagging him about who and what he isn't.

➤ If you want to be treated like a queen, treat your husband like a king. Don't wait on him to do what you want before you do the right thing. Keep planting seeds you would like harvested and watch God.

Shei Atkins

Prayer

Dear Heavenly Father,

Your Word says that a wife is to respect her husband and that is my desire. Help me respect my husband. I don't want to be guilty for creating walls between my husband and me. Lord I admit, it's hard to respect my husband when I'm mad at him. But my desire is to please you and I can't please you if I'm disrespecting my husband. Father forgive me for disrespecting my husband and not appreciating him. Give me a fresh love for my husband. Remind me of all his good traits and help me not to focus on his faults. Grant me insight to meet my husband's needs and humble myself so that I may be able to fulfill his needs. Help me to respect my husband intellectually, physically, and verbally. Allow my husband to see the positive changes I make and I thank you for turning any damage I've caused my husband around and cause it to work out for my good. Allow our marriage to change the course of my family's generations and break the curse of divorce, adultery, and separation. In Jesus name, Amen.

10

What Submission Really Means

I have learned that everyone does not cook spaghetti, gumbo, and other dishes the same way. Everyone cooks their meals differently. To be honest, some people's food tastes horrible and some people throw down in the kitchen. I believe submission in marriage is the same. Many people have correct views and some have wrong misconceptions on what they think submission means. One thing I can tell you is that you cannot have a healthy marriage without godly submission. This ingredient should NEVER be left out. Lack of submission has ruined many marriages. Submission and respect run along the same lines, but I wanted to discuss them individually. Let's look at the definition of submission. Submission is defined as "the condition of being submissive, humble, or compliant." Based on the dictionary's definition, submission is a condition or state that you choose to remain in. Let's move on to the scriptures.

Don't be selfish; don't live to make a good impression on others. Be humble, thinking of others as better than yourself. Don't think only about your own affairs, but be interested in others, too, and what they are doing. Your attitude should be the same that Christ Jesus had. Though he was God, he did not demand and cling to his rights as God. He made himself nothing;* he took the humble position of a slave and appeared in human form. And in human form he obediently humbled himself even further by dying a criminal's death on a cross. (Philippians 2:3-8)

Wives, submit to your husbands as to the Lord. For the husband is the head of the wife as Christ is the head of the church, his body, of which he is the Savior. Now as the church submits to Christ, so also wives should submit to their husbands in everything. Husbands, love your wives, just as Christ loved the church and gave himself up for her to make her holy, cleansing her by the washing with water through the Word, and to present her to himself as a radiant church, without stain or wrinkle or any other blemish, but holy and blameless. In this same way, husbands ought to love their wives as their own bodies. He who loves his wife loves himself. After all, no one ever hated his own body, but he feeds and cares for it, just as Christ does the church— for we are members of his body. "For this reason a man will leave his father and mother and be united to his wife, and the two will become one flesh." This is a profound mystery—but I am talking about Christ and the church. However, each one of you also must love his wife as he loves himself, and the wife must respect her husband. (Ephesians 5:25-33)

Love is patient, love is kind. It does not envy, it does not boast, it is not proud. It is not rude, it is not self-seeking, it is not easily angered, and it keeps no record of wrongs. Love does not delight in evil but rejoices with the truth. It always protects, always trusts, always hopes, and always perseveres. Love never fails. (1 Corinthians 13:4-8)

According to these scriptures, you can see that submission is a two-way street. No marriage will remain healthy without submission from both the husband and the wife. The bible really makes it plain and simple by commanding all believers, including husbands and wives, to submit to the needs of each other. But I really want to focus on the wife submitting to her husband. I am assuming that you have married someone who has been approved by God or either you are single and you plan to marry in the near future. You may be married to a man who thinks submission is controlling his woman. That type of thinking is foolish and is very hard to submit to. Submission and control are not the same at all. Submission is voluntary; control is not. Remember that a relationship between a husband and a wife is a natural representation between Jesus and the church. Do you see Jesus abusing the church? Do you see Jesus forcing the church to do anything? The same way God commands us to offer our lives to Christ; we are to do the same for our husbands. Submission is so significant because it is the behavior of a wife who wants to win her unsaved husband over to Christ.

Check this out.

In the same way, you wives, be submissive to your own husbands so that even if any of them are disobedient to the Word, they may be won without a word by the behavior of their wives, as they observe your chaste and respectful behavior. (1 Peter 3:1-4)

Now do you see the significance in submission? If your husband is not saved, be an example to him and pray for him. Don't irritate and push him away by nagging him. You do not have to say a word when you walk in submission. Your godly actions will win him over. Submission is one of the best gifts you can give to your husband because it offers him the security he needs to be able to open his heart to you. Submission speaks loyalty, respect, and honor to a man. Many Christian men want to serve their wives when they see her going out of her way to make sure he is happy and taken care of. Your submission to your husband will only be as strong as your submission to God. The same thing applies to your husband. Your relationship with each other will only be as strong as your relationship with God. So it is very important that you are where you need to be spiritually. It takes a strong and mature woman of God to submit to her husband. Submission is literally a willingness to daily die to selfishness to give yourself over to serving and pleasing your husband. You are not off the hook from walking in obedience even if your husband is not fulfilling his part of the equation. Don't let women who disrespect their husbands influence you to disrespect your husband. Don't let them make you feel weak about serving your husband. I have heard women with my own ears say they will never submit to a man. That mentality is guaranteed to keep you single, or cause your marriage to be short-lived. Submitting to your husband is in no way an act of the weak. It is actually an act of the strong and can change your marriage around tremendously for the positive. While they are turning their men's hearts away from them, you will be winning your man's heart over. Do not wait until your husband emotionally disconnects from you to do what's right. Treat your husband like a king now. I'm reminded of a lady who I counseled who needed some advice because she had disrespected her husband for so many years that she pushed him away. He became detached and now she is trying to win him back over. Even though they live in the same house, they have become strangers. You never want that to happen.

Never assume that just because your husband is a Christian, that he will always be there. And never think that you can mistreat him consistently over a period of time without it affecting the marriage. A man will not give his heart to a woman who is not submissive and does not respect him. Listen, you may have grown up in a home where you never saw submission in effect. All you may have seen is disrespect. You may have seen a lot of divorce in the family and never had a good marriage to look up to. You can break out and be the example. Break generational curses in your family and change the course of your family's future generations. Show your family and people around you that you can have a good marriage. Good marriages are not an accident and do not just happen. You have to work at it. Make the decision to submit to your husband. Submission is a condition that you choose to remain in. Picture submission as an invisible bubble that you can walk into. Once you walk into it, lock it up and never come out. The enemy, life circumstances, and problems in the marriage will try their hardest to shake you up and knock you out of your submission bubble. Don't allow your circumstances or what your husband is not doing make you go back to your old ways. Remind yourself that every time you come out of the bubble, it is going to negatively affect your marriage. Let a happy, wholesome, and successful marriage be your motivation to stay in the submission bubble. Submission gives you influence with your husband. Submission is attractive to your husband. It is the very key to your husband's heart. Submission is the road you take that will lead you right to a happy and successful marriage. Now that you are in your submission bubble, let me give you a few tips and things you can do to show your husband unconditional love through submission.

20 Submission Strategies

1. Wear hairstyles you know that your husband likes. They usually tell you which ones they like.

2. Wear makeup that turns your man on. Ask him his opinion on the makeup you wear. The clown face is not cute and a

ghost face with a darker neck is not cute. Ask him about the eyebrows you draw on. Some women look like they're always saying "Huh" with their eyebrows like that. He might not want to hurt your feelings and tell you. So ask him his opinion and if there is something about your makeup that he'd like you to change.

3. You know the outfit that your husband compliments you on all the time? Wear similar styles to that outfit often. You are your husband's eye candy and he wants everyone to see what he's working with.

4. Wear perfume your husband likes. That cheap perfume is not going to cut it...especially if you spray too much on your neck and he wants to kiss your neck while making love.

5. You know your husband likes sex, so wear some sexy lingerie that you know he likes. Who wants to pull off sagging panties?

6. Take care of your body and try to stay in shape. Men are visually stimulated.

7. Never go a day without expressing love to your husband.

8. Assure your man that he is the only one you want.

9. Involve him in every single detail of your life. Share it all.

10. Remain faithful to your man.

11. Walk in forgiveness.

12. Focus on the positive in your man and do not major in his minor issues.

13. Don't give anything or anyone more time and energy that you do not give your own husband. Make pleasing your husband a hobby.

14. Willingly take care of your husband's sexual needs. Even God wants a cheerful giver.

15. Make it a habit of doing what your husband enjoys.

16. Encourage your husband and respect his decisions.

17. Cover your husband in prayer.

18. Allow him to teach you without getting defensive. I'm still working on this one.

19. Always respect your husband

20. Show him you need him.

The same level of obedience required to submit to God is the same level of obedience required to submit to your husband. Remember that your husband is your spiritual leader even if you feel he is not acting accordingly. You have the power to turn your marriage around by walking in submission. Always choose actions that bring life to your marriage. To God be the glory in your marriage and may the reflection of Jesus be seen in it by remaining pure and holy before him.

Points to Remember

- ➢ God commands wives to submit to their husbands as unto the Lord.

- ➢ Submission is a form of loving your husband.

- ➢ Submission is the key to your husband's heart.

- ➢ You can win an unsaved husband over to Christ by walking in submission.

- ➢ Your submission to your husband will only be as strong as your submission to God.

- ➢ Submission is a daily choice you make to unconditionally love your husband by willingly dying to selfishness. You have the power to turn your marriage around by relentlessly walking in submission.

- ➢ Submission is not an act of the weak, but an act of the strong.

- ➢ Imagine submission as an invisible bubble that you can walk into. Go inside and never come out. Life will try to shake you up to make you come out of your submission bubble. Prayer and trusting God will give you the strength to remain inside.

Prayer

Dear Heavenly Father,

I acknowledge your presence in my life. Thank you for choosing me and calling me out of darkness into your marvelous light. My eyes have been enlightened concerning submission. I understand that submission has the power to make or break my marriage. I ask that you cleanse my heart and mind from any negative attitudes concerning submission. I ask that you would forgive me for trying to control my husband. Forgive me for treating my husband as if he was my child. Forgive me for not respecting and reverencing my husband like you command in your word. Forgive me for criticizing my husband in front of the children, friends, or associates. Lastly forgive me for not respecting my husband's masculinity, dreams, and decisions. I admit I was wrong and I ask you to create in me a clean heart and renew a right spirit in me. Forgive me for allowing selfishness and how I feel to influence how I treat my husband. I love and appreciate my husband. From this day forth, I commit to loving, respecting, and submitting to my husband. My desire is to please you, Father. Help me submit to you first, and then let an overflow of that love spill over to my husband. Help me to never allow anything to come between me performing my wifely duties. I choose to make my marriage a top priority and thank you for anointing me to be a loving and submissive wife. I recognize that I have the power inside of me to turn my marriage around. I praise you, trust you, and thank you for resurrecting my marriage. In Jesus name, Amen.

About The Author

"Get a Man, Keep a Man" could not have been a more appropriate title for the first book written by this phenomenal author, singer, songwriter and fitness trainer. The inspiration behind this incredible work, no doubt, was birthed from extensive experience. A native of Houston, TX, Shei Atkins married her childhood sweetheart, Drathoven, (who is also her musical producer) at the tender age of nineteen. These two soul mates are the "apples of each other's eyes" and are currently enjoying an almost nine-year run of marriage going forward.

After releasing three independent albums on a national scale, and having been a featured vocalist on the Grammy-nominated compilation released a few years ago, the twinkle behind Shei Atkins' star certainly shows no signs of fading. Shei has worked in the recording studio with industry giant, Beyonce' Knowles, and the likes of platinum-selling rap artists, Lil Flip, Paul Wall and Chamillionaire. She has also traveled the United States and abroad while sharing the spotlight with such notables as Mary J. Blige, Mary Mary, J. Moss, Kirk Franklin, Avant, Tonex, Fred Hammond, Tank, Mario, Lil Mama, B5, Trey Songs and even an international European tour with the Grammy Award-winning Kelly Rowland. While it soon became obvious that National Recording Artist, Shei Atkins, was a worthwhile asset to all of these endeavors, the demand for her electrifying, yet warm presentation, became more and more in-demand and Shei even went on to be featured in one of America's largest publications, VIBE Magazine.

The social networking sites quickly climbed from buzz to ring regarding Shei's honesty and transparency about love, life experiences and relationships mixed with healing and faith, all themes in her music which have led to her current fame. In response, young women from all over began to reach out to her in pursuit of answers and solutions to the everyday issues of life. Using her heartfelt earnestness, Shei began speaking outside of her musical elements and has since traveled as a motivational speaker and formed an inner-city youth group named "Shei's Girlz." "A Heart for the People" definitely describes her in more ways than one. While balancing an already busy recording and touring schedule, Shei, the young woman of "many hats," yet managed to add "fitness trainer" to her growing list of titles. She works well with training clients for a healthier lifestyle, physically, mentally and spiritually.

Shei is an all-around, down-to-earth individual whose light has touched masses around the world. Many of the quotes from this book have already helped many in passing, and the power of fusing them all together for this composition is bound to create a dynamite explosion.

To contact the author's email:

sheiatkins@gmail.com
Or visit:
www.sheiatkins.com
www.myspace.com/sheiatkins
www.facebook.com/sheiatkins
www.sheifanclub.ning.com

Please include your testimony
or help you received from this
book when you write.
Prayer requests are welcome.

Thank You

I would first like to thank God for my wonderful life and family. I thank God for every storm He's carried me through and I would like to thank my husband Dra Atkins. Dra, thank you for loving me the way God loves me. Thank you for supporting and encouraging me when I didn't think I could make it. Thank you for believing in me when I didn't believe in myself. And thank you for being the greatest husband a woman could ever have. I would also like to thank Tony Gaskins Jr. for believing in me. Tony, you saw something in me and helped me pull it out through sharing your wisdom with me. As a result, this book was birthed out of me. Coaching me was very unselfish of you and it means a lot to me. Thank You. I would also like to thank Michael C. Mayes for all his help with the bio and synopsis. You are truly special. I would like to thank my mother and father for everything you've taught me and for being great parents who never gave up on their children. I would like to thank every person who has purchased this book to help make it a success. Last, I would like to thank all of my friends and fans for supporting me this far. I'm truly grateful and you are appreciated.

Made in the USA
Lexington, KY
06 July 2010